THE WAR LIBRARY

A SUBALTERN'S WAR

CHARLES EDMONDS

ANTHONY MOTT LIMITED
LONDON

Published by Anthony Mott Limited 1984
50 Stile Hall Gardens, London W4 3BU

First published by Peter Davies Limited 1929
Third impression revised by the author 1929

ISBN 0 907746 38 1

Printed in Great Britain by
Richard Clay (The Chaucer Press) Ltd
Bungay, Suffolk

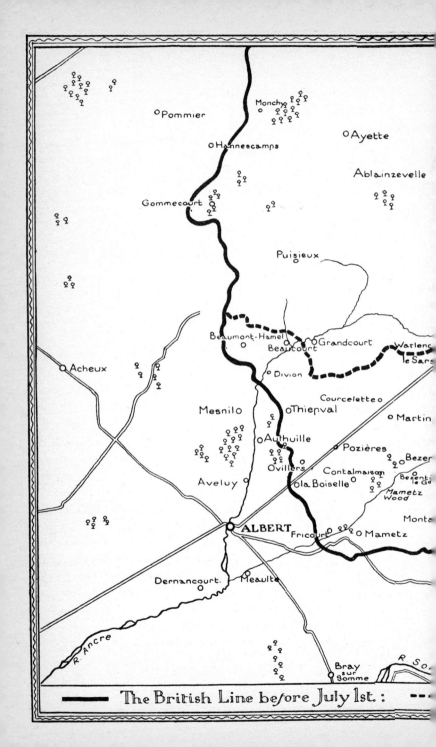

The British Line before July 1st :

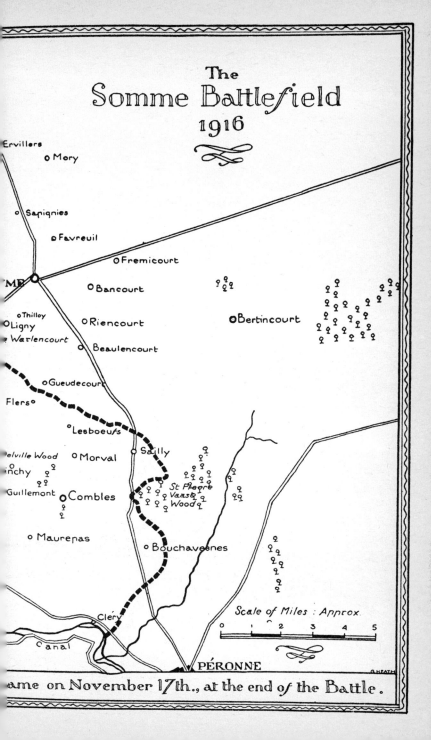

The
Somme Battlefield
1916

Ervillers
o Mory

o Sapignies

o Favreuil

o Fremicourt

MR o
o Bancourt
o Bertincourt

o Thilloy
O Ligny
o Riencourt
e Warlencourt

o Beaulencourt

o Gueudecourt

Flers o

o Lesboeufs

elville Wood   o Morval   o Sailly
inchy
St Pierre
Guillemont   O Combles   Vaast
Wood

o Maurepas

o Bouchavesnes

Clery

Canal

Scale of Miles : Approx.

0   1   2   3   4   5

PÉRONNE

G. HEATH

...ame on November 17th., at the end of the Battle.

PREFACE

Fifty-five years ago, when I prepared an account of the First World War for publication, I described my book as the "memoirs of a romantic young man, with candid accounts of two battles written shortly after they occurred." This was to imply that in 1929 I did not necessarily still subscribe to the notion of the War which had carried me through the trials of 1916 and 1917. Nor do I now imply that the view I took of my "romantic" youth at the mature age of thirty-two is the view I would take as an old man who has survived a second world war and much else besides.[1]

Since my book has been thought worth reprinting after so long a time, I ask my readers to admit the claim I formerly made for its distinguishing feature. I tried to unpack and discharge my memory of "everything that remained in my mind, adding nothing and omitting nothing" —that is, in respect of the two main incidents. I wanted to establish the record, rather than to make some particular ethical or aesthetical impact. My book, I wrote, differed from other warbooks in being "not a record of impres-

[1] See *Soldier from the Wars Returning*, by C. E. Carrington. (Hutchinson's, London, 1964.)

9

sions received but an account of how a young soldier occupied his time, and a list of the duties he was called on to perform." The greater part of it was composed in 1919 and 1920 when the events described were fresh in my mind, and the whole was checked from the home-letters I had written in the trenches, and from the war-diaries of the battalion in which I served. I could also draw upon some scraps and sketches which I had attempted to write during the campaigns, though none of them seemed to me fit for publication. Since I am dealing in history, not in *belles lettres*, it may be that I should now prefer the rough drafts, if they had survived, to the version re-written after the War, which irks me today for some literary flourishes that I thought rather fine in the nineteen-twenties.

I wish I could still draw upon the description of the bloodiest battle in British history, the opening of the Somme Offensive on 1st July 1916, which I wrote in a front-line dug-out, that very evening when the fighting had died down. It is not extant, though I have a version reconstructed not long afterwards. In February 1917, I began to collect material for the factual war record I intended to produce some day. In these times when reticence is out of fashion it seems strange that I was deterred from publication for ten years by unwillingness to commit the indecent exposure of describing my own feelings; and when at last I allowed my memoirs to appear in print I was relieved to find that my military record was regarded as respectable. So far has realism prevailed over romance in treating of war that no one any longer supposes every honest soldier to be an unwavering hero; and the change in public sentiment may be judged by the reception I expected and the reception I got. My book was heavily reviewed in Britain and in America, and was even trounced by some critics on the grounds that I was a brutal unfeeling militarist. This, I own, astonished me.

No one, I think, has made a comprehensive study of the emergence of anti-militarism in all the belligerent countries as a consequence of the miseries and disasters of the First World War. In 1914, the hysteria of the moment was of another kind; what was then significant was the abandonment by the liberals in all the European countries of the principles to which they had previously adhered. Those were the days when H. G. Wells wrote chauvinistic articles against Germany, and when the Fabian Socialist, Rupert Brooke, proclaimed his delight in dying for his country. It was the radical intellectuals who were deluded, not the diplomats nor the soldiers; and it was their eventual return to their earlier principles that released the phenomenon called 'disenchantment' or 'disillusion'. No professional soldier is likely to be 'enchanted' by the prospect of war, since its miseries are more familiar to him than to other men; and the only disillusion experienced by the diplomats was their horrified realisation that the game had been taken out of their hands.

Young soldiers who enlisted without expecting hardships and danger must have been foolish indeed; and any who misjudged the nature of army life were quickly introduced to the realities of the situation by the old soldiers. It can only have been a very stupid, insensitive, young man who did not concentrate his mind, sometimes during the long months of military training, on blood and wounds. We were pretty well prepared for the horrors of war by the time we came to face them, and though, for my part, I have never been able to work the Battle of the Somme out of my mental system, nothing happened to me there which could be described as 'disenchantment' or 'disillusion'. It was what I had bargained for.

The reader will notice that the phase of the War described here is the dull, hard, slogging, middle period, when the forces of the combatants were evenly matched and when, on the Western Front, the British Army was taking the strain. The "feel" would have been different in the early days when no one, not even the Regular Armies, knew quite what they were in for; and different again towards the end, when the massive American intervention had made ultimate victory certain for the Allies. The very beginning of a campaign, at the moment of truth when soldiers who have known only sham fights suddenly turn to deadly weapons, has an intensity unlike any other human act. First battles, such as Lexington, Bull Run, Mons, Dunkirk, have an element of surprise which gives them a dramatic character that is not repeated. A wary, cynical, professionalism soon replaces the ignorant *élan* of the opening moves and, by the time that main forces are engaged in the decisive struggle, there is little room for enthusiasm. Trench warfare had been established more than a year in France and three sustained attempts to break the deadlock had already been bloodily repulsed before I reached the front line. The time was long past when anyone could take a romantic view of the War as a whole. No one could describe the ponderous movement from the training camps to the Front with the phrase that Rupert Brooke had chosen for the sudden change from the pettiness of peace to the grandeur of war—"swimmers into cleanness leaping".

Nevertheless each new age-group has its "romantic young men" and the four of us who joined our battalion in the trenches facing Gommecourt Wood, in January 1916, were as personally committed to adventure as any knights-errant in an old romance. We were volunteers, we thought our cause was just, and we had been long preparing for the testing-day. It is at this point that I produce Dr. Johnson's pregnant saying: "every man thinks meanly of himself for not having been a soldier, or not having been at sea." We welcomed danger and we expected the worst. No one today can have any real notion of the First World

12

War who does not appreciate that, rightly or wrongly, wisely or foolishly, we did these things with our eyes open.

The wisest among our national leaders had from the beginning harkened to the warning of Kitchener that the War would be long and hard, even though optimistic youngsters had eagerly set their hearts on a smashing victory. Repeated failures in 1915, not only in the West but in every attempt to open a new front, threw us back upon Kitchener's appreciation. He had been right and we could not expect a decision even within the three years of his forecast. When the expected term had come, and gone, in the autumn of 1917 it needed no profound study of political arithmetic to observe that the time-schedule must be extended. The defection of Russia postponed our chances of victory, while the counterweight to be supplied by America could not take effect within the next year or two. We well knew how long a time was needed to create a New Army and a munitions industry. When Kitchener's three years seemed to be drawing out indefinitely, the trench-joke of the period ran: "When will the War end?" "They say the first seven years will be the worst!"

This was the testing-time (as I wrote in 1929) "when the grimmest struggles took place, when no eye could see a glimmer of light, when all pity was "choked with custom of fell deeds", and when the weaklings began to fall away. Then the unorganised nations fell into ruins, and then the undisciplined characters failed at the test. An irrational cry, like the cry of a hurt child, against the harshness of the world, broke from the over-sensitive and the temperamental; but once begun the agony had to be endured . . . As the soldiers grew war-weary, so their doggedness grew. The end of the War was the test of character." It was behind the lines, among the non-combatants that the phenomenon of "defeatism", a willingness to escape from the horrors by any sacrifice or surrender,

13

appeared. Armies rot from the roots. I do not speak, in terms of morality, of the way in which soldiers ought to behave in a better-conducted world; but in terms of historic experience, the way in which they do behave. Among British writers to whom the label "anti-war" is attached, the names of Siegfried Sassoon and Robert Graves are eminent. Both were fiercely critical of the higher command and of the political direction of the war. Sassoon, in particular, was adopted by the left-wing press in London as their champion, whom they tried to publicise as a pacifist martyr. But Sassoon, like his friend Graves who served in the same regiment, was an exceptionally brave man and no defeatist. Both of them saw the War through, and reserved their comment, the sustaining factor for both being *esprit-de-corps,* a passionate addiction to their regiment and to their comrades whom they would not fail. The younger and simpler author of *A Subaltern's War* could take this enthusiasm a stage further; like so many young men he enjoyed being a soldier on the whole.

If there had not been hundreds of thousands who were still determined to go forward, whatever their degree of disgust or exhaustion, the British Army would have collapsed into anarchy in 1917 as the Russian Army did, and as the French Army so nearly did. This is the phenomenon which has not been understood by the critics. Why did the soldiers go on fighting, after so many failures and defeats? Why and how did the survivors of the Somme and Passchendaele persist in their solidarity, defeat the German onslaught in the spring of 1918 and break the Hindenburg Line in the final autumn of hard and bloody fighting? They could not have reached their goal if they had at all resembled the woe-begone weaklings with no confidence in their leaders who are described in the books produced by the school of "disillusion".

But the proud, dogged, tense spirit of the soldiers of

14

1918 did not at all resemble the image in which they have been represented. Most of the war-books which attained such popularity ten or twelve years later, with the honourable exceptions I have mentioned and some others, were written by non-combatants who observed war externally from behind. Two books by reputed American author's, Hemingway's *Farewell to Arms* and Cumming's *Enormous Room*, may be quoted as samples of the low morale that prevailed behind the lines. Both are books about men with safe assignments far out of danger, "cushy jobs" as we called them in those days, who decided to shirk, and boasted of their moral failure. Fortunately, such men as are described in these books were rare exceptions. None of the books I have mentioned had one tenth of the effect of Remarque's *All Quiet on the Western Front*, the best-seller in most western countries in 1928 and 1929. I notice that I then described it as a "highly coloured romance" about "disgusting and contemptible characters". It does not lack interest as a classic example of what can be done to float an inferior article into popularity by a worldwide publicity campaign which, as all advertising men know, can be done only on the crest of a wave of public opinion. *All Quiet* satisfied the demand of readers in 1929 for dirt about the First World War, during the antimilitarist reaction that broke surface ten or twelve years after the War had ended. But the mood of 1929 was quite unlike the mood of 1917, and the enthusiasm of post-war civilians for Herr Remarque's best-seller was not widely shared by ex-soldiers who, if they applied their critical faculty, could hardly fail to notice that this author knew all about "wangling" and "scrim-shanking" and looting in the back-areas but became less convincing, the nearer he drew to the battle-field. One was left with a lingering doubt whether he had ever been there. It was a book about the rear, not the front.

In those days the front-line soldiers of 1914 to 1918 formed a secret society which knew neither rank nor nationality, and it is not extinct even in these days when we survivors are old men, the youngest not less than eighty-five. Get into conversation with a stranger of your own generation in any of the combatant countries and, in five minutes, you would know whether he was a front-line soldier or not. It was impossible to simulate the style and slang of the trenches if you had not been there. False pretences were instantly exposed by some assumption or claim that lacked verisimilitude. Like a masonic password, a village-name, an allusion to some detail of trench-routine, a reaction to an anecdote, revealed a man as your comrade, as one who shared the unforgettable, indescribable experience, or as an impostor.

The front-line soldiers resented attempts by back-area non-combatants to claim admission to their circle, and were contemptuous of the patronage of civilians. Fifty years after the outbreak of the First World War reunions and rallies of old soldiers are held, not only by regiments or divisions, but by "Old Comrades' Associations" in hundreds of townships and of business firms. The comradeship of the trenches, later to be misconstrued and parodied, was real in the sense that the old soldiers held together and grumbled over the secret that could never be revealed. During the War they had hated the patriotic hysteria of the civilians, and after the War they rejected consolations offered without understanding. They had "done their bit" and didn't want to discuss it with the uncomprehending. To me the mood of 1929 with its pacifist emotionalism, its crocodile tears over the dead, and its absurd attempt to make the military commanders the scapegoats of a bellicose human race, seems more irrational than the warlike mood of 1914 when the issues were clear, when men had no doubts about the duty that lay before them.

16

In 1914 I was a very young soldier, so young that I have sometimes wondered whether the whole problem may be summed up by saying that I was a juvenile delinquent, who wanted to gang up with the other boys, to demonstrate my manhood, and to be allowed to indulge a taste for anti-social violence. It would be insincere to exclude this factor and inadequate to overweight it, if only because many respectable men, old enough to be my father, fought through the War; if only because I enlisted again in 1939. Better, perhaps, to abstain from arguing and let the story make what effect it can. This is what I thought about it at the time.

When this book was first published and many of the characters were in my social circle I thought it best to disguise all names in order to be free to make candid comments on their behaviour as well as on my own. Many are now dead and all are scattered. May I ask any survivors about whom I have made unkind remarks to forgive me if they should recognise themselves. To authenticate my narrative, in case anyone should care to trace the two or three lines allotted to each of my battle-episodes in the official histories, I now reveal that I served in the 48th Infantry Division, commanded by Major-General Sir Robert Fanshawe (1863-1946), the 143rd Infantry Brigade, and the 5th Royal Warwickshire Regiment. My commanding officer on the Somme was Lt.-Colonel G. C. Sladen (1881-1930) who afterwards commanded the Brigade at Passchendaele. My commanding officer at Passchendaele was Colonel W. C. C. Gell (1888-1970), to whom I am obliged for help when this book was first published, and for many other kindnesses.

"Charles Edmonds" [C. E. Carrington]
July 1984

CHAPTER I

1914—1916

BEGINNING OF A SUBALTERN'S WAR

§ 1

> *"Then a soldier,*
> *Full of strange oaths, and bearded like the pard,*
> *Jealous in honour, sudden and quick in quarrel,*
> *Seeking the bubble reputation*
> *Even in the cannon's mouth."*

THE war caught up the author of these memoirs, a boy of seventeen, out of a country vicarage. I lay in a hammock and ate plums—too many plums—in a garden full of delphiniums which seemed to go on flowering week after week in that splendid summer of 1914. We started a grand offensive (there was a family) against wasps' nests, and were not very brave. One of the girls was frightened of the dark even more than of wasps, and when I walked down the lane with her to a late party I shamefully showed that a very dark lane made me feel creepy too. I might have gone to school for another year, but one day there was a crisis in Serbia reported in the morning paper, and I said wilfully that I would enlist as a soldier to fight for the Serbians. My uncle said: "You'll do nothing of the sort."

19

Suddenly this crisis came out of the newspapers into real life and even into the village, where the butcher and the stationer stood at the street-corner being oracular for long periods which were punctuated by the arrival of trains from London, bringing special editions of the newspapers, full of lying rumours.

On August 4th, a roasting afternoon, my uncle and I went for a walk and met a sweating soldier on a bicycle looking for his colonel's private house. When we directed him we learned that he carried the mobilisation order, and late that night a notice at the post office told us that war was declared. The meetings at the street-corner with the butcher were feverish with excitement. No day passed in which spies were not shot in the Tower, or battleships sunk in the North Sea. The Army and Navy performed astonishing feats in which we all believed. The Hidden Hand of the Kaiser was everywhere. In our village there was a little barnstorming troupe of actors who played a repertory of melodrama in a wooden theatre, which happened to be burned to the ground a day or two after the war began. Over the hot ashes stood the proprietor of this gallant little enterprise, complaining of nothing, but protesting that the Germans must have done him this ill turn. I wonder where the chance of war whirled him away.

At the vicarage our offensive against the wasps was maintained. We also bought maps of all parts of Europe and stuck little flags in them to mark the position of armies. My cousin had gone to the war, and the chauffeur and I planned to follow him. After several false starts I enlisted as a private soldier in a Kitchener's Army battalion and went into training in the Midlands. Before long my other cousins departed to war work and war marriages, until the family was scattered and holidays at the vicarage came no more.

In this story of the war there will be no disenchantment. No corrupt serjeant-majors stole my rations or accepted my bribes. No incompetent colonels failed to give me food and lodging. No casual staff officers ordered me to certain death, indifferent to my fate. After the war was over a fashion set in for decrying the efforts and defaming the characters of all those in authority in the war, but we never thought of such things in 1914, at least not in my regiment. Never were such splendid fellows assembled, never was such keenness to make order out of chaos, never was such blind hero-worship as we paid to any soldier who would teach us his trade.

At first I was billeted in a cottage in a midland town with three other men, a clerk, a commercial traveller and a gas-fitter who was also a Communist. I "mucked in," that is, shared blankets and food and cleaning-kit, with the gas-fitter. We drilled every day for long hours in the park, at first in mufti and then in rather gaudy blue uniforms. Does anyone now remember that Kitchener's Army wore blue because there was not enough khaki to go round? We used to make a game of standing outside a picture palace pretending to be commissionaires and misleading enquirers. It was great fun being a private in Kitchener's Army, but for one absorbing problem. When should we get to the front? The winter passed; 1915 dragged on and still we stayed in England drilling. One was oppressed with fear that the war might end before we reached the front. Some men deserted to enlist again in regiments which they fancied might sooner go abroad. For my part, I got my uncle to pull some strings and was given an officer's commission in another regiment. If it was fun to be a Tommy, it was ten times more fun to be a subaltern in Kitchener's Army. There was scope. A thousand things had to be learned and taught to willing men. Leadership, the most heady and intoxicating draught for a young man, became

21

a duty and a delight. We vied with one another in caring for our platoons, and, off duty, carried ourselves with no end of swagger, each trying to be the devil of a fellow.

In the summer of 1915 the regiment went to France. It was a grave shock to find myself left behind as too young. From the glory of a service battalion, where everyone assumed that everyone else was keen and efficient, I was dropped into the wretchedness of a reserve battalion populated by all the failures and the faint-hearts, where the stout fellows had only one interest in life: to escape to France. Here a truth came to light. The further from the sound of the guns, the lower was morale. In the most dangerous places you found the best men. Not till December 1915, when I was eighteen and eight months old and had been a soldier for a year and three months, did I manage to get to the front. On Christmas night I crossed in a troopship to Havre, being extremely seasick all the way, and went for a few days to the base camp on the hill at Harfleur. With three other subalterns I was then sent "up the line" to join the regiment in trenches some miles north of the Somme. This was the moment for which we had waited so long, and happy were we to arrive at the village close behind the lines where the quartermaster lived.

§ 2

Four very excited young men left their billets that January morning to join the battalion "in the line." It was far more like stepping out from the pavilion to bat for the first time in a match, than like waiting with horrid anticipation at the dentist's door. The war was still a picnic, or seemed so. The battalion was in "cushy" trenches, that is to say, posted in an easy position where the enemy were not too near nor the gunfire too frequent. It was fine sunny weather, and if the front line trench was thigh-deep in mud, that mattered little, for it was almost all abandoned. Six platoon posts were drained dry and kept clean by arduous digging and pumping, and in each of them resided a serjeant with fifteen or twenty men to hold the front, while most of the battalion lived in dugouts scooped into the bank of a sunken road three hundred yards behind. Here was battalion headquarters, where the colonel, the senior major and the adjutant lived in great state, with a sentry before the door paraded as in Aldershot itself. Not far away behind the company commanders, each in a timbered cavity under the bank which he shared with his three or four subalterns. By day one officer of each company was forward "in the posts," the others dozed and gossiped, hunted rats with a terrier, or watched the aeroplanes pursued across the zenith by distant tiny puffs of smoke, which meant shrapnel from the "archies," the anti-aircraft guns. Sometimes there would be "strafing"; our guns would arrange a shoot on some suspected enemy post and provide free entertainment for our lazy sightseers; or it would be the Germans who rained down storms of shrapnel; or flights of "whizz-bangs"—small shells that came like thunderbolts out of a clear sky, so swift that you were not warned by the noise of their approach—broke up our merry party and sent the sightseers scurrying down the dugouts. This was all comedy, and taken as such. Everyone applauded if the guns scored a fair hit on a tree or house and brought branches or tiles crashing down. To stampede a group of loungers, or scatter a party of diggers was a good joke for which one gave due credit to "brother Boche." If he hit battalion headquarters or drove an inspecting general ingloriously to earth, that was the best joke of all. Only on rare occasions did the comedy turn to tragedy, for to the bitter end of the war it remained the greatest wonder that so much ammunition could be expended without hurting anyone but the taxpayer.

The first of these catastrophes which I saw gave me a truer impression of the danger. After two or three weeks at the front I was watching, as orderly officer, the giving out of tea from a great cauldron, or "dixie," to a queue of men standing in the sunken road. Without warning a whizz-bang pitched on the bank and burst among us flinging tea and men in all directions. In an instant there was a scramble for the dugout. Some men staggered and fell. Dizzy and scratched, but not hurt, I found myself holding a big serjeant who was hit in the thigh, and was collapsing in my arms. Behind us on the ground a man lay groaning, but it was some seconds before I dared turn and look, afraid of what horror I should see. I busied myself dragging into shelter and bandaging the serjeant, while others attended to the groaning man. In two minutes there was no sign of the disaster; in twenty all the men off duty were lounging again in the lane, cleaning rifles, picking the lice off their shirts, laughing and joking, just as before. But I never knew the same carefree feeling in the sunken road again. I found myself inclined to cock an eye or an ear perpetually in the direction whence that shell had come.

By day there was really not very much to do. Sometimes working parties could be organised, if the trench to be dug or drained was passable by daylight. A memorable day it was when two of us had drained a long communication trench called Fifth Avenue, penning the mud and water behind a temporary dam of clay, in a dead end—a grand game of mud pies for a boy on a spring morning. Then came news that the brigadier and his staff were coming up the trench. Now trenches wind in curious zigzags lest enemy guns should be able to rake them, shooting along them in a straight line from end to end. The brigadier, though only a few yards away, could see and know nothing

24

of our doings round the corner. We broke down the dam, releasing a flood of liquid slime, knee deep, glutinous, stinking, which swept him away. No gilded staff officers appeared after that to interrupt our innocent ease in the front line.

Mostly the world slept by day. When dusk fell, allowing movement over the top, a hundred strange activities began on both sides of No Man's Land. Troglodytes emerged from their burrows in the sunken road to relieve the platoons in the posts, to bring up rations from the village, to dig and wire in pitchy darkness. Heavy labour at a score of trades in awkward places must be relentlessly performed without showing a light or making a sound. Some skilled officers and men crawled, boy-scout fashion, to listen and observe near the enemies' lines; some wrestled like the slaves that built the Pyramids at dragging baulks of timber, coils of wire and engineering tools by main force to the line; some with torn and bleeding hands struggled Laocoon-like to twist and strain new strands of barbed wire into the entanglement a few yards in front of the posts. The ceaseless watch was doubled, and sentries strained their eyes through the darkness, peering over the parapet into the open field (the Racecourse, they called it) bounded two hundred yards away by the German wire entanglement, behind which in equal darkness and silence the unseen, unheard enemy watched and sweated and laboured in just the same way. A sniper's bullet cracked now and again across the Racecourse at some suspected movement, but no one took any notice. For some reason a frenzied burst of shell-fire would scatter the workers for an hour and disorganise a night's routine, or perhaps all would be silent save for mutterings and rumblings from the livelier parts of the line fifty miles away. Some nights in the trenches were deathly still, enlivened only by uncanny greenish rockets, Verey lights, which the

Germans fired over No Man's Land in great profusion.

When the dawn broke, everyone stood to arms. Sentries and their reliefs, working parties and sleepers in dugouts, rose, took their rifles and stood in their battle positions watching the sky grow grey. Snipers fired a round or two to hearten themselves; machine-gunners loosed off a couple of hundred rounds to drive away belated wanderers from the top of the opposing trenches; men who had toiled all night yawned and stretched, listening to the eerie whining of bullets overhead. Then came rum issue. An officer with the jar under his arm passed round giving half a gill of raw rum in a mug to every man, an occasion of much crude jesting and good humour. The sun was now up; the word was given to stand down, and but for drowsy sentries all the world retired to sleep in its clothes for the day. Across the road the Germans were doing just the same. One might be weeks in the trenches without seeing or hearing anything of the enemy except his shells and bullets. A thread of blue smoke from his trenches at breakfast time when you too were cooking bacon over a charcoal brazier; a flitting figure in the distance caught in the glare of a rocket; a head and shoulders, seen from the sniper's loophole, leaping past a gap in the enemy's parapet; a rumbling of wheels from his wagons far behind the line at night; these and the ghostly Verey lights alone certified that his trenches were occupied by human beings too.

The brigade, of four battalions, had two battalions in the line, one in support living at a little château a mile from the trenches, and the fourth resting in peace at a village two or three miles back. Every eight days they all changed places. Month in, month out, from the autumn of 1915 to the spring of 1916 this "tour" of duties went round. Nothing made much difference save when in February heavy snow made all open air life unbearable, and in March when the Boches favoured us for a week with their

26

"travelling circus," a group of batteries that visited various parts of the line with concentrated bursts of shell-fire. In these days I was very happy. This was *Life*, and if one was occasionally frightened out of one's wits, a sudden fright never did a young man any harm. One night I took part in a highly organised raid on the German trenches and thoroughly enjoyed it, although it was a total failure costing twenty casualties. To lie breathless in the German wire with a storming party of volunteers, armed with clubs and made invisible in the darkness by having our faces blacked, was a splendid adventure; and who cared for the rifle bullets stabbing through the dark point-blank, as the Germans drove our wire-cutters from their task?

In April the whole brigade marched back twenty miles to rest in a delightful village bright with apple blossom among green downs. Never was any picnic, any country holiday so enjoyable or so enjoyed. Not to be dirty, not to be hungry, not to be overtired, these were all a man asked, and only he who knows weariness, hunger and dirt can appreciate their removal. "Rest" in the Great War meant stiff military training all the mornings and games in the afternoon. We young fellows enjoyed the parades and were mustard keen, though we naturally grumbled about one thing and another. We slept under a canvas sheet in an orchard overlooking the valley, ragged one another like schoolboys, and spent much time eating and sleeping.

One day there was a reminder. Three men were blown up in a trench mortar accident before the whole brigade. "Mais, que voulez-vous? C'est la guerre; à la guerre comme à la guerre," as the French peasants replied to every objection.

When we went back to the trenches a new spirit was abroad. May and June 1916 mark to the historian a crisis in the war. The Irish Rebellion, the Battle of Jutland, the death of Kitchener in quick succession filled the English newspapers with vague alarms, which were reflected still more vaguely on the armies in France, where the initiative was passing from the Germans to the Allies. All the spring the Germans had been hammering at the French lines round Verdun, and their blows were now losing weight. The German offensive having spent itself, the allied offensive was soon to begin. Every recruit could see new batteries springing up in the night among the woods, violent activity in the skies, for spring brings in war something more than primroses and swallows. Trenches and roads were doubled and redoubled. More men came into the line, filling our familiar rest-billets with strange regiments, thronging our roads with guns and wagons, crowding our dugouts, and leaving us only a narrower section of the front line to hold. The trenches were no longer "cushy." Raids took place almost every night to see what damage the guns had done by day; and what we did to them the Boches sought faithfully to do to us. These activities steadily increased, the noise growing daily louder and life getting harder, until the famous First of July, the opening of the Battle of the Somme, the most violent and ruthless battle in the history of the world.

We did not attack that day. It was our part to loose off a cloud of smoke and gas which blinded a section of the German line, making a poisonous screen to cut their defence into two halves which could not support each other. Mr. Masefield in his book, "The Old Front Line," has described that day, which it is no part of my purpose to describe here. All the enthusiasm of two million volunteers trained for two years at home and in quiet trenches was focused on this day when the citizen soldiers, Territorials and Kitchener's Army, met the army of Frederick the Great, of Blücher, of Moltke, very old at war, on equal terms.

What we saw of the battle was a failure. World-shaking bombardments which made our little memories of trench warfare ridiculous, hurricanes of shell-fire, hurled on us by the Germans in retaliation, glimpses through the smoke of attack and counter-attack on our right and left, came to nothing, till the regiments which had advanced in the morning crept back in the evening to their own lines, leaving three-quarters of their men dead or wounded in the German trenches. We were thirteen days in the line without a relief and without shell-proof dugouts. We lost seventy men killed and wounded by shell-fire; about one in seven of our numbers.

I do not remember that we were in the least discouraged by the failure of our part of the battle. On July 5th we were withdrawn from the line to a village five or six miles away where we bivouacked in a grassy dell. It was a wet summer and not pleasant for sleeping on the ground under little open wigwams of brown canvas, yet morale was very good, better than usual. Every day *communiqués* were posted in the camp telling of the progress in other parts of the battle, how Fricourt, Mametz and Montauban had been captured, and of the heavy fighting at La Boisselle. At this time, too, we were thrilled by the news from the Russian front, where General Brussiloff was winning in Galicia the last victories of the Czar's empire.

Every day a company or two would be roused at dawn to march deviously up to the trenches, avoiding observation as far as possible by the German kite balloons hanging in the distant sky—faint specks that reminded me of caterpillars hanging by a thread, save that they hung upwards in the sky, not downwards like caterpillars. Near the front line there was much work to do making new trenches or repairing old ones destroyed by German shells on July 1st. The companies who stayed in camp drilled in the morning and idled in the afternoon. One day someone organised a cricket match, officers versus serjeants. In the evenings there was a troupe of pierrots, the divisional concert party, performing in a barn.

On Sunday at Church Parade the whole brigade attended, and we were horrified to see how few were left of the two battalions which had "gone over the top" on July 1st. But this was not a melancholy occasion: it was enlivened by a speech from Lieutenant-General Sir ———, of whom so many comic stories were current. He commanded the whole Army Corps of 80,000 men, and was a very great man indeed. Nothing irritates the soldier so much as heroics, for which this general was renowned. He strode into the midst of the brigade and poured forth such a wealth of what Stalky called "jelly-bellied flag-flapping" that our own general blushed for shame and the rear ranks shook with ill-concealed giggles. The great man retired convinced that he had made a good impression.

From such circumstances we were whirled away by the fortune of war into the vortex of the battle about La Boisselle. Until the moment came there was little speculation about our fate, for one learnt to live for the day only during the war.

The episode, of which I wrote a complete account in the days when it was fresh in my mind, began in the middle of July 1916.

CHAPTER II

AN ADVENTURE ON THE SOMME

§ 1

ONE day I went out early with a hundred men and the usual instructions—to report to the Royal Engineers at a point given me by map reference. I had two junior sub-alterns with me and we marched by platoons a hundred yards apart, a formation we always used in case of being shelled. We went up the road to the Dell, then by a cart-track along a hollow across the plains, always with an eye for enemy balloons that might be watching, to a row of old gunpits near the sugar factory. There the Sappers took my men, dotting them on various jobs of trench repair, and thereabouts through the maze of old French trenches I wandered supervising. Soon after midday we started back on our five-mile walk home, and on the top of the rise saw the battle flare out again over Mailly-Maillet to the south—the roaring of the heavies, the distant metallic thud of the shrapnel, the white puffs of smoke that merged and blended into a heavy grey pall.

As we approached the Camp there seemed to be an air of excitement, but no one could tell me definitely what was astir. The Colonel had gone to Fricourt on a "Cook's tour" of last week's battlefield. The Second in Command was out somewhere and we had had an order to move. Bickersteth, my company commander, had been whirled off to Division for orders. We were to get ready. And even then he came flying down the hill in a car. We ran to meet him.

"We've got to move by motor bus in half an hour," he shouted. "Get the servants to pack the mess-box, Edmonds," he went on, turning to me, "and Edmonds," as I turned away, "will you see to the Lewis-guns? And hurry the men up."

I dashed away, with my head full of heroics, almost ashamed of these trivial duties.

"And Edmonds," he shouted after me, "go round the lines and see they are tidied up."

Then followed half-an-hour's frenzy—rolling of blankets, loading of Lewis-gun carts, strapping of valises, finding fatigue parties for the Doctor, the Orderly Room, the Pioneers, the stores, the transport, passing rumours and orders, improvising, cursing, sweating. And as the lorries drew up to the camp and the men were falling in, here came C. Coy, who had gone out at three in the morning on a far more distant job than mine and were now returning dead beat. Never mind. It was three in the afternoon and time to go. They must turn to and pack up, while we loaded our stores, and jammed our men on the lorries, tighter than fowls going to market in a crate.

At last we started over the chalky dusty downs. I sat beside the driver, who told me we were going to Bouzincourt.

Along the Route Nationale from Doullens to Albert I hardly realised what was coming. My mind only treated the affair as a doubtful adventure. It was the same feeling that I had on my first day at school—a blankness, a numbness of intellect. But for that curious hungry feeling, the coming battle seemed only like an adventure in a book. "Realise," said I to myself, "you know what shelling is in a trench. You have sat and shivered as the crumps fell closer. Now you are going to be shot at in the open field. You have heard the bullets crack round your ears. Next time you will have to face them. There will be no taking cover. And you are going to meet your enemy face to face."

But I could not frighten myself. There was already glowing in me, and I think in most of us, the first exaltation of battle. I was uplifted in the spirit, and could only watch and almost gloat over the warlike preparations around. For we were moving along dusty roads that passed by camps and wagon-lines, shell dumps and hospitals, and from the villages came curious throngs of men with a steely light shining in their eyes, an exalted look which I often noticed again after a battle. They were the men who had come through the furnace.

Through these days of battle one lived in an elevated state of mind which a doctor might have defined as neurosis. The strange sense of dual personality which comes to so many people at moments of high tension was hardly ever absent. There was an arguing realism, a cynical side to one's nature that raised practical objections and suggested dangers, and against it there strove a romantic ardour for the battle that was almost joyful. While the mind took sides and disputed with itself, the body seemed numb and void. An emptiness almost like a physical pain tormented my bowels: the naked fear, basest of human emotions, fighting its way up from the subconscious and finding a voice in that part of my mind which reasoned and realised. Sometimes one was swayed by the delight of achievement, sometimes dragged down by fear. Always the struggle within, fought behind the dark curtains which screen the hidden springs of conduct, was more real than

33

the physical struggle without, and the practical details of life passed by like an illusion.

We halted behind the chalk ridge above Bouzincourt in an hour or so, and disembarked. There were some minutes of inaction as the battalion formed up in a field beside the road. Packs were taken off, rations were issued and we lay down to await orders. Our mess-box had little in it, of course, but we ate some bread and tinned salmon and felt a little better. Bickersteth suggested gently enough that more care would have been wise before such a move, and I admitted one point of advantage in his fussing. Further I remembered here that the gramophone had not been brought. Bickersteth had seen it, though, and had left it in charge of the Pioneers who did not come with us. As a matter of fact we never saw it again.

Now a fit of depression seized me. I was cramped, dirty, and hungry, and annoyed that I had failed in my duty as Mess President; and to occupy my mind, I got ready all the things I should want in "fighting order." Less cheering still was the rumour that we were going up to La Boisselle, a recently captured village, of which a map was issued to us—just a rough sketch showing the present position of the lines, which seemed very confused. But soon we had definite orders to move at nine, which was dusk, to the white house on the cross-roads at La Boisselle; so an hour or two of peace was left us.

That road was like a pageant. The quieter men lay down, but the younger ones, officers and men, ran about like children to see the sights. Someone saw a monoplane coming, a queer flat squarish thing. It didn't look British. It came straight for us. Was it a Taube? There was a little flutter of pleasant excitement. It dived. It swooped straight at us, crowded in the field. At last we saw the Allied marks on it. It came down faster till the pilot leaned over and waved to us. We could see him smile. Then as the men

34

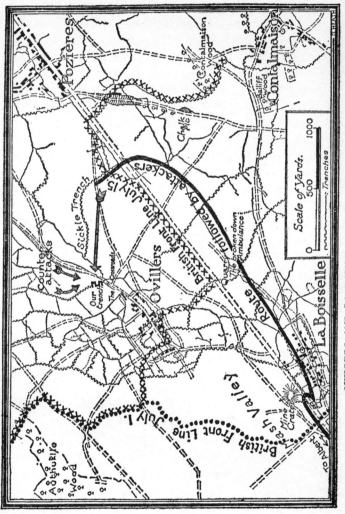

OVILLERS AND LA BOISSELLE, JULY 15TH, 1916.

scattered and his screw was whirring right upon us, he lifted again, cleared the trees along the road by a miracle and sailed away. He, too, was exalted with the battle.

Then two slow tractors lumbered into view drawing long Naval guns. "Six-inch," said someone. "Twelve-inch," said another, and a little crowd dashed to the roadside to see them.

Before they had gone a party of heavy loose-limbed men in a slaty grey uniform came marching over the brow headed by a horseman. Their faces were pasty with fatigue, the growth of several days stood on their chins, their eyes were dull and they walked despairingly. Someone saw the gleam of red on their caps.

"Allemans," he shouted, "come on, lads"; and away went another group to watch them with friendly curious eyes, with the look of men who watch a caged animal.

But the greatest excitement was when with jingling harness two squadrons of cavalry trotted by, English Lancers and then Indians, with gleaming equipment and clean new helmets, on their way to High Wood where they would charge through the broken German lines.

" 'Struth," shouted a man of ours, "it's Cavalry. We've got 'em on the run." And all the battalion believed it.

Last, as we were forming up to go, two subalterns of another regiment came up to me. They appeared to have had their turn and were interested in ours.

"You'll be all right," they said comfortingly, "we've got the Boche taped. You just go over the top and rush for it. If you don't get there you're only wounded. The Boches are shooting very low. Most of our chaps were hit in the legs."

We marched off dragging our Lewis-guns by ropes attached to little hand-carts. At the top of the hill smoking was forbidden, and we marched down the other slope into Bouzincourt. For the time fear had gone. In the dusk many men came out and looked at us from the mud houses that lined the road.

"Their companies are as strong as our battalions," said a man bitterly by the roadside. I realised then a new thing, we were fresh troops compared with these weary ones. Our long purgatory before and after July 1st was nothing to the hell they had endured.

Next a new type of man rushed out and spoke to me, a tall, gaunt man in a slouch hat.

"What lot are you?" he asked me. "You're the best looking crowd I've seen down here."

That was a proud moment: my regiment had been praised by an Australian. Even an Englishman does not often volunteer a good opinion of another regiment.

We marched down a long slope with transport lines in a hollow on our right, and into the dingy suburbs of a town that I took to be Albert; but I began now to think more of the guns, for on all sides we became aware of heavy batteries hidden in heaps of ruins or among trees, and every few moments one of them would fire. The moon was brilliant as we marched under the railway arch into the deserted town. Most of the walls and roofs were standing, but the moon showed the windows as squares of blackness, where no glass was throwing back her beams.

In one street stood an empty factory with its girders twisted and battered into writhing shapes of rusty iron, and its productions, which appeared to be sewing machines, lying in useless heaps among the wreckage. Then

37

came a large, barrack-like girls' school, empty and deserted; beyond that the street curved round into a wide space where the houses were levelled to the ground and straggling weeds grew over their ruined heaps of brickwork; but nothing caught the eye then save the huge mass of the basilica on the left, that church which lost its modern pretentiousness in the dignity of its fate, and over which towered the far-famed campanile bearing on its summit the golden virgin of Albert. The colossal figure, struck by a shell, was bent forward and stretched horizontally over the street. I had seen it before from the top of Henencourt hill, but never had I been so profoundly moved as in passing under its outstretched arms that caught the gleam of the moonlight a hundred feet above us. Something of the dramatic fitness of the silhouetted mass against the sky, topped by this golden figure, seized the imagination of the long columns who marched below, speaking only in whispers. The melodrama of it rose strongly in our hearts.

We turned into the Rue de Bapaume and marched between lines of squalid houses, over a railway crossing and out of the town. The proximity of war came more to our notice. The battery of six-inch long guns that we had seen earlier in the day was halted on the road here, and near them we turned into a field on the right. The last house of Albert—the Red House, we called it—was just behind us.

The battalion formed in mass, and the ominous order was passed down to dump packs and change into fighting order. Now the cold fear clutched at the bowels of men who had missed a night's sleep and a day's good food. I began to congratulate myself that I had made ready my fighting order at the last halt, and plumed myself above those who groped in the dark for food and utensils. The time was so short that many were without what was needful. Some order was established, in the dark, for it was unsafe to show a light; packs were heaped in piles by

38

companies; the transport and the quartermaster-serjeants stayed and we fell in again. After much delay the battalion shook out into platoons at intervals of fifty yards along the straight broad road that led like an arrow to Bapaume. It rose gently up the long slope to Tara Hill, flanked on either side by a ditch and a line of stunted scorched trees. It was more uneasy work marching with these little groups. The very fact of this scattering gave cause for fear, as this formation would not have been used unless shell-fire was expected. The night was growing darker. The moon had gone, and from the deserts that might be dimly descried on either hand came strange noises, the stamping, snorting, shuffling and jingling of unseen horses, the roar and flash of invisible guns, and a multitude of sounds faint and distant but unexpected and cloaked in darkness. There were many halts on the road: I had to run forward to see that touch was maintained, to run back and bring up the rear, endlessly to wait with nerves on edge while slow coming messages were passed down explaining incomprehensible faults and checks in the column. It felt lonely to be more than a few yards from some friendly group of human beings. At last progress ceased altogether. Other traffic was thick on the road; a battalion in front, unknown to us, was holding up the column; a battalion behind recklessly marching in fours was pressing on our heels. Regardless of all the rules of march discipline they came past us at a swinging pace, smoking and whistling, with a cheery colonel marching at their head.

"Excuse me, sir," I said, when he came abreast of me; "you're in view of the Boches here. It isn't safe to smoke, and you're breaking up our column."

"I can't help that," he said, "I'm going on."

And they marched on. There were now three battalions jammed on the road, and before we should be hopelessly confused and cut off from our head, we too closed up our column from the rear, until three parallel battalions in fours were halted near the crest of Tara Hill.

I was intensely nervous. If any firing had begun we should have been thrown into utter confusion, for a high bank on our right and a well trodden morass some feet below us on the left, would have prevented any ordered deployment. We waited fretting for an endless period of time. It was no easier when a sharp bombardment began a mile in front of us. Somehow the way cleared and we went on over the crest and down into a valley with a shattered copse on our right. This was clearly the battle zone, for the metalling had vanished from the road and we marched over stiff clay sodden after the heavy rains. The wilderness to right and left seemed drearier and more silent, and we began to meet stragglers coming down from the front line. Two mud-covered men came by carrying petrol tins for water, then a stretcher party bearing a dark young man whose face seemed set with a greenish pallor, then a solitary wounded man with a bloodstained bandage on his arm, nursing his wound and crooning to himself with low hysterical sounds, sobbing and cursing.

"Halt at La Boisselle," had been our orders, "take the turning half right at the cross-roads and halt at the first house on the left—a white cottage."

We came at the bottom of the valley into a new country. It was a desert of broken chalk—ditches, holes, craters, mounds and ridges, dry and thinly overgrown with weeds, and all interlaced with rusty strands of wire. The road vanished in this waste, hard by a great mountain of gleaming white chalk on our left.

At this point, quite unexpectedly a 4.2 howitzer shell came jubilantly sailing over and crashed into the chalk beside us with an air of almost human satisfaction at having surprised us. There was a waver along the ranks, for manifestly we were getting lost, and the march was suffering yet another check. Then came another shell falling closer, a crescendo of sound rising to a high note as it reached the top of its trajectory, falling, as it came near, to a low sibilant roar. It burst with a crash and a buzz of flying splinters, close by, and we cowered into shell-holes and under banks. Then shells came over one by one at regular intervals. It began to dawn on me that the head of the column must be in La Boisselle, that this was our objective.

"This is going to be a bloody business," I said to Suckling, who was beside me, for he was marching at the head of his company, I at the rear of mine.

"Well, it won't help us if we get the wind up," he said rather pointedly. Those were his last words to me, for at that moment I saw Bickersteth in front of me directing the company down into a trench on my right.

"Get the men under cover," he shouted to me, and I ran about, finding shelter for groups of men in ditches and craters near by. Crouching in the dark as the whine of the shells and the crashing explosions came, the men spread about off the line of the road. Soon we saw on our right an extensive trench system, into which the C.O.[1] was marshalling the companies. We herded the men down into a shallow trench across our front and slowly moved along it into a maze of turnings. Richardson brought his platoon along over the open trying to break in ahead of me, and as second in command I warned him off. He subsided grumbling, for he was old enough to be my father and obeyed me unwillingly.

The trench we followed was wider now and deeper, a ten-foot furrow through the chalk, blocked here and there

[1] The Lieutenant-Colonel commanding an Infantry battalion is generally referred to as "the Colonel" or "the C.O." (commanding officer).

by the smashed doorways of dugouts and the ruin of fallen traverses and bridges, for it was German ground and had suffered much from the effect of our bombardment. The two companies in front of us led off into different sections of the system and at last a rough area was left us. We pushed on and found a deep mine dugout with two entrances. Company Headquarters and one platoon went in here, and the rest of our scanty hundred were stowed away in nooks and corners of the trench under the shelter of low bridge traverses, or in the mouths of abandoned or damaged shafts. Some made shift to scoop into corners of the trench wall, and undercut little caves for one or two. The remainder were accommodated two deep sitting all down the steps of the dugout. So we settled for the night.

The bombardment slackened for an hour or two and we improvised a meal. There was little but bread and bully beef, but the servants were indefatigable. I felt triumphant on finding that of four officers, I alone had brought a mess-tin and a knife and fork. We shared things somehow, and Bickersteth, Richardson and Wells settled down to sleep. This was the first German dugout we had seen, and I felt the romance of our position too strongly to sleep just then. It was a long, narrow chamber with a steep stairway leading up to the trench at each end. It was lined with rough planks and had room only for two rows of home-made bunks—wire netting stretched over wooden frames—a shelf which could be used as a table, two or three chairs, and the narrow gangway from end to end. There was a strong, stale, fetid smell of sweat and decaying paper and old clothes, permeated by the solid flavour of the earth that lay 15 feet thick above our heads. The floor was littered with dry cakes of mud, scraps of paper, old messages and documents, English and German, rags and fragments of food. There was a general feeling of filthiness.

A thousand messes had spilled and soaked into the table; gutterings and soot abounded where candles had stood on any projection of the woodwork; the beams were shining greasily from the touch of grimy hands; there was nothing in the room that was not smeared with muddy finger-marks.[1] Men were packed close into this corridor and lying comatose in every corner. Their limbs, flung in careless attitudes, lay across each other as they crowded on the beds or huddled on the floor. By the dim candlelight I could specially see the bristles showing on my neighbour's chin, for his beard grew very strongly. He was dozing fitfully with a pained expression on his face. I felt angry with him for he seemed so careless about it all.

With a terrific detonation a shell burst in the trench above.

" 'Struth," said the man on the top step of the shaft, shifting uneasily and crouching into cover. I looked round. Everyone else in authority looked invidiously asleep and unconcerned. It made me angry to see them all snoring heavily when there was trouble outside. Ought I to go up and see if all was well? It felt very safe and comfortable down here.

"How are you getting on up there?" I shouted up the shaft.

"All right, sir," a voice replied, "but they're dropping very close." There was a tinge of envy in the voice too. It was all very well for me, it seemed to imply, shouting up from the bottom of the dugout. I hesitated a moment longer. Why should I go up? Bickersteth hadn't put me on duty. He'd just gone to sleep and left me. I forgot the work he had done, the responsibility he had taken, that the whole organisation of the move had fallen on him when the C.O. had been away earlier in the day.

[1] I became lousy for the first time in my life in this dugout and blamed the Germans for it.

43

Crash! came a shell right at the mouth of the shaft. The roof rocked; the air of the dugout vibrated; the pressure of it seemed multiplied tenfold.

The man on the top step flung himself down a step, cursing and cowering into the already overcrowded shaft.

There was no help for it. I picked my way up the steep flight of rough steps, stooping under the low roof, climbing over the limbs of drowsy men who squatted two on each steep and narrow stair. As soon as I began to move the fear dropped from me a little, and sitting near the mouth of the shaft I fancied myself a hero. "Let them sleep," I thought, "I know my duty. I'll take the point of danger." .Certainly the men seemed to appreciate it, and we fell into conversation.

"How are things going up here?"

"Not up to much, sir."

"Anyone been hurt?"

"Ain't heard of any, sir, but it ain't for want of trying."

"This is a pretty bloody place, isn't it?"

"Yes, sir. How long do you think it'll be before we get relieved?"

"Relieved! Why, we haven't started yet. We may have to go over the plonk in the morning."

Silence. Another shell burst a little farther along.

"Everyone all right?" I shouted along the trench.

But before any answer came, we heard a low faint cry far down to the right—a blood-curdling sound, neither a moan nor a wail, but something between the two, a cry that rose and fell a little for three seconds. Then silence again.

Summoning all my courage, I went out of shelter and moved along to the right. A man crouching under a fallen traverse spoke to me.

"It's a policeman, sir, in C company. That last one got him, sir."

44

"Is anyone looking after him?"

"Yes, sir. The stretcher-bearers have gone along that way."

It was no business of mine, I thought, and was turning back when yet another shell came, giving the least of warnings. It burst before us after so short a roar of coming that the brain had no time to appreciate it.

"By gad! That's a quick 'un," I said, the beads of perspiration standing on my forehead.

"It's about a twelve-inch, I reckon, sir," said the man; "comes at yer like a whizz-bang too."

"Somebody told me there was a high-velocity gun that fired on this corner. I don't think it's as big as that, though. They do have five-nine high-velocity guns," I said; "it's firing at damned close range anyhow."

I moved about the trench. Only a few more shells came over and those at longer intervals, till at last they ceased for the night. It was cold and damp, so that the men lying in the open, under crazy lean-to's of wood or scooped-out holes in the trench wall, could sleep little. Those in the dugout shaft were dozing uneasily when after an hour or so I decided to go down. I was more than ever jealous and angry with the sleepers below, none the less because I knew the men had noticed it, and were giving me more credit than I deserved for the night watch. I had been longer than any of the other officers in this company, and the men knew me better than they did Bickersteth. I had no idea of the tactical situation, no conception of our position on the rough sketch that was my only map, no means of judging whether an officer need be on duty all night. Deciding to risk it, I crept down the shaft over the grumbling drowsy forms that filled it, and finding a vacant bed I slept till daylight.

When I woke the dugout was dark save for a faint light that was thrown down the shaft. There were fewer men asleep on the bunks, and looking round I saw that Bickersteth had gone. I was damnably stiff and dirty, so rolled out of the German blanket that I had slept in and went up into the trench. Dawn was breaking grey and misty; there was no shelling. Bickersteth was bustling about setting the men at work improving their shelters or cooking breakfast over little fires.

"Come on, Edmonds," he shouted with joviality; "what have you been doing? We've been up for ages."

When I protested that I had been out half the night, he failed to be as grateful as I hoped and only asked why. My account of the shelling satisfied him a little. Finding work to do we separated, supervising improvement, re-organising and talking to those men who had been in the worst condition during the night, until there arrived what seemed to me a miraculous meal of tea and bacon.

Afterwards we walked out under cover of the raw fog to look at the situation. The beat of gunfire, so persistent for the last fortnight, was very near, but no shells came our way. Two men came unmolested over the top with petrol tins of water from some water-point. We talked of improvements in the crannies and shelters where many of the company had slept, for Bickersteth thought we might spend some days here.

"Where's this village they talk of?" I asked him. "What's happened to La Boisselle?"

"This is it! Look! I'll show you where we are on the map."

"Then where are the Boches now?" asked I, looking vaguely towards the east. "No wonder we couldn't find the village last night." There was not a house, not even a ruined wall left standing and the very lines of trees that flanked the road had been blown out of existence. The only landmark was a high rim of white chalk, fifty yards in diameter, like the crater of a volcano, into which the road vanished.

"Gad! Look at that mine-crater!" I said.

"Far's I can make out," went on Bickersteth, looking learned over his map, "this is the old German front line in front of La Boisselle. Then that," he pointed to a straggly line of orchard trees half a mile away across a low valley, "must be Ovillers. The Boches are still there. The 17th are in front somewhere in the line. We'll have to go up and attack this long curved trench on the right of Ovillers. Think I'll go along to Headquarters now and see if there 're any orders. I believe we're attached to the 125th Division."

Presently Sergeant Coke, a fair-haired, pleasant-mannered young man, drifted into conversation with me.

"There's a lot of dead Boches along here, sir," he said cheerfully.

This roused my interest, for curiously enough, though I had six months' service in France and had often seen men hit, it had always been in well-ordered trenches, where casualties were soon disposed of; and I had never seen a corpse.

"Come along, sir," said Sergeant Coke, leading the way over the holes and hummocks of chalk. "When we were up at Messines they lay about thick. I pulled the teeth out of one of them and made a necklace of them. All the chaps used to rummage round them for souvenirs. Careful, sir, look out for this wire! Lord! They used to smell in the summer when the flies were bad. Do you know what we are up here for, sir?"

"No," said I, a little disgusted.

47

He chattered on in a silky civilised voice. "The chaps are pretty tired, sir. Some of them didn't get any sleep at all last night with the shelling, and then they'd been up since two o'clock yesterday. Captain Mayhew didn't like it a bit. He said C company had touched lucky as usual. They had a man hit in C company."

"Yes," said I, "he was a policeman."

"Look at this, sir!" gloated Serjeant Coke. 'This' was a rusty tangled framework made of iron stakes and barbed wire of the kind which soldiers call a 'knife-rest.' It had been struck by a sixty-pound trench mortar bomb of which the stem lay close by. In the middle of the tangle, as if the wires had been carefully twisted round it, was a bundle of rags. They were grey and of fine texture, like my own khaki, obviously the ruins of an officer's uniform. It was only when I noticed two smartly booted and gaitered legs in tan leather protruding from one end of the bundle, that I realised it was anything more than rags. No other sign of humanity was visible.

I thought of that smart German subaltern, a man perhaps very like me, crawling carefully over his parapet, as I very often had to crawl over mine, to see how the wire was standing the British drumfire. There was a patch of shadow under the knife-rest where he could lie unobserved. Then the barrage fell in thunders and lightnings. The air was full of reeking smoke and whining fragments of steel. He would try to crawl back as the British bombardment was directed on his belt of wire, but the sixty-pounder fell and killed him in the thicket of iron thorns unseen.

But Serjeant Coke was enjoying himself. "There's some good ones over here," he said, "in the big crater. Come on."

I went fascinated.

There were several men standing about making little fires of splintered wood, for the morning was too thick to give the enemy a view of us. Two or three were looking into the mine crater when we reached it. This was not the 'Glory-Hole,' the great crater of La Boisselle, nor yet the equally great one on the Bapaume Road, but a small fifteen-foot hollow among many shell holes. In the bottom of it were lying two curious things. They were muddy grey in colour—clothes and boots and faces. They had features, but features swollen till the skin was stretched tight over their brows and noses and cheek bones. They lay, not in picturesque attitudes, but in the stiff unreal pose of fallen tailor's dummies; they looked less human than waxworks; all the personality had faded from their faces with the life. Big men they had been: they had now a horrid plumpness. In awful fact they were bursting out of their clothes.

I felt neither afraid nor unhappy, but fascinated. These things were less like men than the friendly earth to which they were returning. They were unclean. I returned satisfied; I had seen a corpse.

In the afternoon Richardson was sent by headquarters to make a reconnaissance up the line. I went to sleep. In the evening he returned, tired, confused and sick with the horrors he had seen, grumbling like a volcano about to erupt.

"It's just murder up there. Why, nobody knows anything. There are no signs to direct you in the trenches—nothing. We must have walked miles and miles—and the corpses everywhere, horrible—why they don't have them buried I don't know. Young Anderson was with me, he's a good lad—twenty years younger than me though. Why, let me tell you, down here it's a picnic: the corpses up there by the Ambulance are awful. There's a place where there's a sort of broken-down ambulance wagon. It's a sort of open place. If you can find the way there it makes a good landmark."

He looked at me as if he thought I ought to have been chosen to go. Bickersteth reddened instinctively: he hated to send anyone.

"Pshaw! They're all lost up there," said Richardson. "No one can tell you where the line is, or the bloody square-heads. There's one good thing anyhow; plenty of those dead fellows are square-heads. If I had my way I'd kill 'em all—wounded and prisoners. The only good Boche is a dead one—bloody square-heads, that's what they are."

"Did you get the lie of the land in your mind?" asked Bickersteth anxiously. "There's a trench here—look! I'll show it you—got your map? All right, look at this. Here you are, now. Most likely we're going to attack this curved trench running out from point 66."

"I don't know about that," Richardson continued doggedly, "I can find the way to that broken-down Ambulance. Everyone uses that for a landmark. I couldn't tell where point 66 is. Of course, no one's given me a proper map, they wouldn't. No system—no system at all. And I tell you, you can't find the way about up there. The trenches are all smashed to hell. There's nothing but shell holes and dead men—horrible!"

"Ought to take a compass and map," chirped Bickersteth. "Set your map! Can't go wrong!"

So the day wore on. Richardson grumbled; Bickersteth fussed; Wells sat nervously; I sulked, while the servants produced meals from nothing in particular.

Next morning the fog held, but the air felt drier. When I went out the guns were cracking and roaring through the mist a mile ahead of us as I had not heard them since July 1st! for though I did not know it, the greatest night attack in the world's history had taken place the night

50

before, and the Fourth Army was beyond Bazentin and Contalmaison, fighting its way into High Wood and Longueval. We were still short of water, which was being brought up by hand in petrol tins, and as I stood and listened to the guns with little Cockburn, the Signalling officer, the colonel's servant came by with a canvas bucket full. We seized on it and washed. It was grey and slimy. The Colonel, the Second in Command, the Adjutant and the Doctor had all been there first, and now Cockburn beat me to it; the bearer and four other headquarters men followed me. No porcelain bath room, hot-towelled and nickel fitted, ever gave such pleasure.

I went for orders to battalion headquarters. There was a road laid with brushwood fascines above our trench. It was thick with parties of men going up and down. I hardly knew that it was the resuscitated corpse of the Route Nationale, Amiens — Albert — Bapaume — Cambrai. It hardly occurred to me that it was our road from Albert. I met Morshead, newly come out to the 16th, very cheerful, and already attached to Brigade as bombing officer. A year later I was to bring him into my trench at Ypres to die.

At headquarters, in another German trench like our own, there were no orders, but magnificent rumours that the cavalry had broken through. I drifted back presently with Heywood, the Adjutant. In our own trench we stood and gossiped. Presently something came towards us with a long, fluttering, whistling sound, like the ghost of a partridge hard hit. It swooped over and fell behind us. Phut!

"Dud!" shouted I in joy. "Ricochet, wasn't it?"

Heywood was dubious and only looked wise. Then came another sound like it, and another shell fluttered and smashed like a rotten egg somewhere behind. Then came more: they didn't explode; they smashed, though with a ring of metal in their tone.

Rotten eggs! No, but there was a smell in the air. It was sweet, pungent, sickly, heavy. Almonds were something like it.

"I think it's gas-shells," said Heywood, grinning.

"Oh Lord," I added without piety.

Flutter, Flutter, Crump! came the shells. Whirra, Whirra, Phut!

The smell thickened and spread and caught at my throat. My eyes began to stream and my nose ran.

"Damn it, it's making me cry," laughed Heywood.

"We'd better try our gas goggles, hadn't we?"

"Right."

We put on the goggles, but they were far from gas-tight.

Whirra, Whirra, Whirra, Phut, Phut, Phut! came the tear-shells thick and fast.

"These damn things wouldn't hurt," chuckled Heywood. "They're too tired."

Whoo—Whoo—Whoo—WHOO—CRASH!

It was a big high-velocity shell that burst in front of us, flinging down showers of hot clods of clay.

"Huh, huh, huh, huh," giggled Heywood, his eyes shining with fun; "that's a good 'un, eh, Edmonds?"

I failed to see the joke.

Whirra, Whirra, Phut!

Whoo-o-o—o——CRUMP!

Gas-shells and crumps came over alternately.

"This is no use to me," said I, "I'm going to move."

I moved till the big gun ceased, and returned in an hour to find Heywood and Lance-corporal Barker still crouched in the same place. The former still laughing, the latter looking unhappy.

Gas-shells still fluttered over by ones and twos, and I felt again for my goggles.

"Those goggles are no good," said Heywood.

"Perhaps they're not," said I, hardly convinced. "How'd you get on? Anyone hit?"

"Yes, one feller up there on top. Not of ours. Direct hit on the head, one of those gas-shells. Poor devil!"

After a pause. "And Corporal Barker here. Huh, huh, huh. Gas-shell hit the trench just behind his head! Ha, Ha, Ha! Thought he was dead, but he wasn't touched."

"Yes, sir," said the corporal more cheerfully, "within a foot of me head it was, sir. If it 'ad 'a' been a whizz-bang 't 'ad 'a' blown me to pieces. Give me a proper headache it 'as too, sir. Give you my word."

"Better go and lie down, hadn't you, Corporal?"

"Aw, I'll be all right, thank you, sir."

The gas-shells hardly ceased all day.

In the afternoon Wells complained that he had no shrapnel helmet. His reward was to be chosen to take all the men in a like predicament up the line to salvage enough of them from corpses. He went against his will and returned in the evening as full of horror as Richardson. I knew, and they knew, that the next horror would be mine.

We were living in the midst of a large population of which we saw little; but now and then a man would pass, with a message, or to a dressing station, or for water or supplies. That afternoon I was sitting in the dugout shaft when a single man came by, asking for brigade headquarters. He was pale, footsore and unsteady; a German helmet hung from his shoulder-strap; his badges showed him of the 17th battalion.

"How are the 17th getting on?" asked I.

"Cut up, sir; been over the plonk," he said slowly.

"No? What did they attack?"

"They call it Sickle Trench, sir."

"Why, that's the one we were going for," said I. "We're in luck."

"We had a real bad time, sir. P'raps you know our

53

colonel, 'e was hit. Went over with the lads 'e did—gloves and stick and all."

"I'm sorry. Did you kill many Boches?"

"Ah, there were a lot of fighting—bombs an' all. Our section was for it. My brother, sir——"

"Hard luck, was he hit badly?"

"He was killed, sir."

"I'm sorry. . . . Can I give you some tea before you go on?"

"Thank you, sir, but I oughter get on with this message. . . . My brother and I have bin together since the division come out."

He shuffled on.

It seemed then that we were to be spared, as our objective had been taken for us. I thought I had already done enough on July 1st. I was to find that we had hardly begun.

§ 4

In the evening Bickersteth and I were summoned to headquarters and I began to feel afraid again. We were the last to come, and found the C.O. already poring over a map, and talking to the ring of officers clustered round, their faces alone illumined by the light of a candle on the dugout table.

"Is that everyone, Heywood?" asked the C.O.

"Yes, sir."

"Right. We're going to do a little attack to-night. Our objective is the cross-roads behind Ovillers. Better look at it on my map—it's the best. Can you see, Suckling? Right. We've got to get there at 1 a.m. It'll be difficult. Jumping-off place is a line drawn from point 66 at right angles to the main road." He talked on as quietly as if he were giving operation orders for manœuvres.

I could hardly listen. A tremendous sense of realisation came over me—I hardly know if it were fear or excitement. I knew just what to do. Attacks I was familiar with, but they were attacks over known ground against imaginary enemies. Fighting I knew, but it was fighting dream battles with visionary foes. That had been a favourite game since I had played at 'fighting the Boers' in the nursery. For the very first time I thought what it meant, to struggle for life with a man of equal wit and training. Not all the strain of six months' trench warfare, of the ordeal of July 1st, of the last two days of preparation, had told me what was the meaning of war, the 'ultima ratio.' In a dream I heard, and in a dream I wrote notes of the plan. The battalion would form here in two waves, would wheel half-left here, would march by this line on the left and would extend and assault here. Our right was guarded by the 17th battalion; from the left the Irish would converge and join us. B company would take the left front.

"What officer are you going to leave behind, Bickersteth?" said the C.O. suddenly.

A wild hope seized me. The second in command was usually left behind. That was myself. Was it a hope or was it a fear? Something in me wished to go with the battalion.

Bickersteth eyed me almost guiltily. "Well, sir," he said slowly, as if it were the basest treachery, "I thought of leaving Richardson behind."

"Good," said the Colonel smartly, "we'll put Edmonds to watch the directing flank."

For a second I was smitten helpless with fear. Then as quickly it vanished, and I found myself, to my own amazement, taking orders in detail as impassively as the Colonel gave them. I was to lead the left flank along an old cable-trench. I was to cross the first trench I came to, and take, hold and fortify, with No. 8 Platoon, the trench junction on the cross-roads. Corporal Turner of C company, with six chosen "stout fellows," was attached to me with orders to strafe a suspected machine-gun post which lay on the left outside our area. Absolute silence was ordered.

The Colonel finished with a stony look. "There will be no retiring," he said. "On no conditions whatsoever is any man to turn back. Let them all understand that."

I was held back when the others left while the C.O. explained my part in detail, drawing me a little sketch of it.

Then I went back to a hurried supper. Wells and the serjeants were summoned to a meeting and their parts explained. Rations, water, ammunition, rum, were attended to; the Lewis-guns were brought out and the clumsy ammunition-buckets served out to carriers. Our cook we left behind to preserve our gear, so back he went with the quartermaster-serjeant and the company cooks.

In less than two hours we were on the move. When the time came for the assembly of the companies along the lines of hollows in the chalk, I was surprised how little I felt afraid. One little incident reassured me still more. An N.C.O. came up and said that Private Eliot wished to speak to me. The man was a mere boy, whom I had known in England, and I felt flattered that he should apply to me rather than to Bickersteth for whatever help I could give. I found him crouched against a chalk-heap almost in tears. He looked younger than ever.

"I don't want to go over the plonk," he flung at me in the shamelessness of terror, "I'm only seventeen, I want to go home."

The other men standing round avoided my eye and looked rather sympathetic than disgusted.

"Can't help that now, my lad," said I in my martinet voice,[1] "you should have thought of that when you en-

[1] I was nineteen years and three months old myself.

56

listed. Didn't you give your age as nineteen then?"

"Yes, sir. But I'm not, I'm only—well, I'm not quite seventeen really, sir."

"Well, it's too late now," I said, "you'll have to see it through and I'll do what I can for you when we come out." I slapped him on the shoulder. "You go with the others. You'll be all right when you get started. This is the worst part of it—this waiting, and we're none of us enjoying it. Come along, now, jump to it."

And he seemed to take heart again.

This incident served to restore my spirits at least, and I found the numb spot in my midriff almost gone. It was about half-past nine, and I was almost enjoying the feeling of responsibility when the long column began to file over the shell-holes through the dusk.

But that walk became a nightmare. I was at the tail of the company, which moved for hours through broken trenches in single file. Just before me the two Lewis-gun teams stumbled along hopelessly overloaded with guns and clumsy ammunition-buckets, swearing and tripping over broken ground and trailing wires. Presently we climbed out of the trench and hurried over a grassy slope that had been little shelled, where there was a light railway. Now and then we passed salvaged equipment and once or twice a corpse lying sprawled by the way. The battalion was already straggling out in the effort to reach that hopeless rendezvous in time. It became harder and harder to keep up the pace with these tired and heavy-laden men. Then we came out on a road that ran along the top of a spur. The high bank on its further side was honeycombed with little shelters dug in the mud, where snoring figures slept huddled under muddy groundsheets. Though the night was clear there was a suspicion of damp drizzle in the air. I rushed forward to try to halt the front of the column for a moment. Bickersteth was nowhere to be found. I

57

pressed on again, but only at the centre of A company could I find an officer, Evers, a subaltern I knew well. He thought vaguely that the company commanders had gone ahead to find the way. At the head of the battalion there was no officer. I ordered them to halt.

"Where is Captain Suckling?" I whispered angrily, not knowing how near we were to the enemy.

"Gone ahead, sir," said a voice, "told us to follow on, and I think we're lost, sir."

"Hell!" said I. "Haven't they left an officer at the head of the column?"

"I dunno, sir," said the voice as if it were quite resigned to its fate and very tired of me. "There's a guide somewheres, sir."

At last I found him, a bewildered private of another regiment, roped in to lead us to Point 66 on the Bapaume Road. He knew nothing: he was waiting for the officer to come back. As we waited for the rear to come up, I asked him about his regiment, and was told a pathetic story of how they had been sent over the top by accident at Contalmaison, and badly cut up because the orderly with the cancelling message never came in time. Then he told me of my cousin in his regiment whom I had not seen since 1914, and how to find his camp at Bécourt.

Soon the situation straightened out and the column moved on. As I dropped back to my place I sent Evers, who was my junior, to take the head of his company with the guide. So the weary march continued through dark winding ways. Climbing over obstacles, squeezing past narrow places, stumbling over fallen wires and *débris*, passing now and again shrouded bundles by the way that sometimes turned with a weary stare, or woke cursing, and sometimes lay still with death. At one point we came out on the main road, wide and clear and empty, flanked with shattered trees, and then went down again into the

58

longest trench of all where the few occupants were men of the 17th battalion. Here, though we never knew it, we were right among the enemy and in danger of counter-attack from almost any side. This, Sickle Trench, was a long curving line that led in the direction of Ovillers from the furthest point of our advanced line.

The pace was now quicker than ever; the companies in rear had dropped right out of hearing, and I was feeling desperate, when suddenly I came, round a traverse, face to face with Thorne of D company, who was pushing and lifting the last man before me, gun, ammunition and all, out on to the parapet.

"Hullo, laddie," he said cheerily enough, and I felt among friends again. But before there was time for explanation he hustled me too out into No Man's Land with a clap on the back and his blessing.

I found myself now in a long slope of rough grass, knee high and tangled, in sight, after all, of what looked like the battalion. Here was the serjeant-major, stumping about on his game leg blarneying the sections into place with his stick, with all the gestures, if not the noise, of the parade ground. But the men were so tired that I found some, waiting in their places, who had fallen asleep here in No Man's Land. Order came out of chaos and I found my place on the left, and Bickersteth not so flustered as I expected. But then we had a severe blow: the pipeline[1] which was to guide our left flank was nowhere to be seen. He sent me along the front to Suckling to change the directing flank, and everyone was warned to go by the right. There went one big responsibility from my shoulder. When I got back to the left I looked with my serjeant across the valley and saw a shrapnel barrage beating right across our path five or six hundred yards ahead.

[1] The line of a straight ditch dug and filled in again, in which telephone wires were buried for protection.

We were gloomily discussing this when with a surge on our right the line went forward. We were "over the top." We went on in the dark, breaking now and then into the double. The exhilaration of that rush of men was wonderful. The two first waves, barely fifteen yards apart, bunched until the sections were almost shoulder to shoulder. The bayonets gleamed in the flashes of the barrage that crashed in front of us. It seemed unbelievable that this torrent of men could sweep upon the enemy unseen.

Down the hill. On. On.

Not a shot was fired.

Now, where the ground sloped up again over broken ground the ranks were breaking and we bunched together.

Someone cried "Extend" and the men threw themselves forward, running now over shell-holes ever closer together. I was no more afraid than if it were all a game. Only where the village was looming up, a black line of ruins and hedges against the dark sky, I glanced nervously, looking for the opening of that flanking machine-gun fire. Surely they must have seen us.

The ground was now torn and furrowed, ploughed into powdery chaos by the bombardment. A battered trench could only just be distinguished in the general ruin.

We broke into a charge and someone behind me tried to cheer. We silenced him, but still no sign came from the enemy.

Over the empty trench, and on. So much for the first objective.

We struggled over mound and crater of spongy soil and reached the road. No sign from the enemy.

Beyond was a high bank, and over that I could see the Verey lights go up from the next German line. But the road was now filled with crowds of panting men. Where was my objective? The cross-roads were blasted out of existence. If that flattened ditch over which I had jumped was my trench, then heaven help us when the machine-guns fired down from the village on our left.

"Get your sections in hand," I shout to every N.C.O. I can see, "and keep quiet, for God's sake." Now to find Bickersteth. I rush madly about in the road and find no officer but Wells—vague and flurried.

"What are we to do?" whispers he, clutching me.

"Go on!"

"No, we've gone far enough."

"Can't stop here," say I.

Then the expected happened. Crack, crack, crack, went the Boche machine-gun, shooting uneasily at this noise from a strange direction, shooting wildly, but showing he had heard us.

I thought frenziedly. Bickersteth must be hit or lost. Had we gone too far or not far enough? The soldier's motto: "When in doubt go forward." At least we could not stay here and be shot down in the cutting. In this supreme moment I was inspired. More and more men crowded on to the road, and half a dozen orders and warnings were bandied about. I drew my revolver and scrambled up the bank.

"Come on lads," I shouted, "over the top."

For one ghastly moment I stood there alone.

It seemed that I was lifted out of myself, and something in me that was cynical and cowardly looked down in a detached way at this capering little figure posing and shouting unrepeatable heroics at the men below. Through the cracking of the machine-gun, and the banging of the barrage, at last I made myself heard.

"Forward! and we'll have the next trench, too."

Then I became aware of a short little fat man standing beside me brandishing a rifle and bayonet. With a common impulse we turned and ran on towards the enemy.

"Who are you?" I shouted. "I can't see you."

"Don't cher know me, sir?" he said; "I'm the serjeant-major's batman."

"Good man," said I, "I'll remember you for this."

As we raced across the short fifty yards of grass a trickle of men and then a rush followed us over the bank. Before us we felt vaguely that there was commotion in the enemy's trench and the Verey lights went up no more.

We were now in the barrage which had seemed to go before us across the valley. I reached the edge of the trench wondering vaguely what I should do if I found a German bayonet-man poised in it to catch me as I jumped.

But the bay was empty, and I landed on the firm floor of the trench just as a shell burst with a metallic bang ten or fifteen yards on my right. This was as good fun as playing soldiers in the garden at home. In a minute there were twenty or thirty men behind me, shouting and laughing as they skylarked round the traverses.

Of course there was no officer or N.C.O. handy. I began to think I was winning the Battle of the Somme alone. Then behind me I noticed the grey head of Corporal Turner, who always reminded me of Baloo in 'The Jungle Book.'

"I've got my six men here," he said rather plaintively. "We can't go for that machine-gun over there, sir. It's miles away. The Colonel told me to stick to you, sir, if we couldn't get at it."

"Good for C company," I shouted, "you're the only section that has stuck together. Take your men down the trench as far as you can to the left and make a bomb-stop and hold that side."

"Right oh, sir," and he went.

Then I rushed along to the right, the way the garrison had retired, but there was no N.C.O. to send to that flank. I put Griffin, an old hand whom I knew to have a head on

62

his shoulders, in charge of two or three men to block the trench by cutting a firing position in a big traverse. Then I went back to my point of entry. The trench was deep and wide, with sheer sides and a firm floor of clay. The traverses were seven or eight feet high and ten feet thick.

I found Serjeant Broad then, an old ginger-whiskered fellow, who had served in the regular army.

"Well, serjeant," I said, "you are the only one here who has been over the plonk before. What do you think of things?"

"Well, sir," he answered deferentially, "I think you're doin' very well, sir. But what about these here dugouts?"

There was a dugout shaft right before us.

"Will I throw a bomb down, sir?"

"No," said I, feeling full of beans, "I'm going down to have a look. Don't let anyone throw a bomb down after me."

The serjeant didn't approve, but I called to Lee, a smart-looking lad who was close by, and we started down the shaft. Lee giggled.

"Lee," said I, "have you got an electric torch?"

"No, sir, but I've got a match somewheres."

So I lit a match and held it well away from me. We crept down the stairway, I with a match and a revolver, he with a bayonet and the giggles.

The dugout opened to the left at the foot of some twenty steps. I slid my revolver muzzle round the corner, gingerly showing the light. Six inches from my hand was the corner of a table on which stood half a loaf of bread, some tinned meat—and there just by my hand an electric torch.

I grabbed it and illuminated the dugout.

Thank God there was no one there. It was bigger,

cleaner and more comfortable than the one at La Bois-selle, and consisted of a corridor about twenty feet long, joining two small square chambers from each of which a shaft led up to the trench. The walls were all panelled and lined with a double row of bunks, on which lay blankets, ruffled from recent use. A greatcoat or two hung on the walls, and (joy!) there were five 'pickelhaubes' [1] lying about. Evidently the Boches had been surprised and run, leaving food, blankets and equipment behind. And no wonder, if they had heard the battalion yelling and swarming over their trenches from the rear.

I called down Serjeant Broad for a council of war. He thought the next thing was to get in touch with the bat-talion again. So we sat down and composed a message with all due military form, saying that we had missed our objective but gone on till we found a safe deep trench with dugouts, quite beyond any of our instructions, and all we knew about it was that by my compass it faced north-east. I sent off Lance-Corporal Vinter with this message to Bickersteth or the Colonel, or any other senior officer he could find.

We were by this time pretty comfortable and altogether pleased with ourselves. The sections were getting to-gether again. I had in the trench with me Wells and about half of the company, a section of A company, and Cor-poral Turner's party of stalwarts. One of our Lewis-guns had turned up, but only Corporal Matthews and two men with it. The flanking parties had not gone far. On the right they had come to a trench junction where they de-cided to stop; on the left Turner had come almost at once to a blank wilderness of shell-holes, where our cross-roads must once have been. So we were crowded into this short section, sixty men in as many yards of trench. Some one

[1] German full-dress helmets of patent leather with brass badges and spikes, souvenirs very much sought after.

had found another dugout on the right, but this I had no time to explore myself.

The night was now far advanced. It was perhaps four o'clock when Bickersteth arrived, full of questions. What was I doing? Why had I overrun my objective? Where on earth had I taken the company off to? We must get ready to go back to our objective, since this was our own barrage firing perilously near to our right flank. He had been left with a Lewis-gun and a handful of men whom he had placed in a shell-hole at the obliterated cross-roads. When he saw the deep trench and the good dugouts, he too wished to stay. Presently the Colonel came over the top from A company, who had settled in that battered ditch behind the road.

"Gone too far, Edmonds," he snapped. "Have to get back to the cross-roads."

"Yes, sir," said I, sorry for the loss of my new playground.

While Bickersteth showed him the good points of the trench, and made a case for staying there, I ran back to the dugout determined at least to find a souvenir. In the shaft I met Wells, and together we seized on the last remaining 'pickelhaube.' We must have been very overwrought, for we stood and wrangled over it, like sparrows over a worm, blocking the trench and holding up the retreat of my little army. In those few moments Bickersteth convinced the C.O. of the advantages of the position, and we were ordered to stay. In the early morning a staff officer appeared over the top confirming the decision.

So darkness faded into dawn, and dawn into damp and misty daylight.

As it was getting light I happened to be on the right, where Griffin's party was struggling with a huge traverse. A man beyond me said excitedly:

"There's someone coming along the trench. I can hear 'em talking."

"Hurrah," I said, "this'll be the 17th." So I jumped on to the traverse and shouted, "Hullo there! Who the devil are you? Are you the 17th?"

Somebody along the trench stopped, and I heard whispering.

"Who are you?" I shouted again, with less confidence.

There was a sound as of someone scuttling up the trench.

"Why, it must have been the jolly old Boches."

We had sent the A company men back to their own trench and organised our own men with sentries on the flanks and a reserve platoon in the dugout, and were feeling safe and happy, when again I heard something going on on the right.

"Stand to," there was a shout; "they're coming!"

My servant and another man who had been hanging about beyond the sentry-post came flying round the traverse.

"Allemans," they said; "they're coming!"

This was a very different matter from running about in noise and darkness. I suddenly thought of Prussian Guardsmen, burly and brutal, and bursting bombs, and hand-to-hand struggles with cold steel. My first impulse was to tell Bickersteth. It was his responsibility now.

'Thud!' went a loud noise along the trench, and the air shook and whined with flying fragments.

I felt myself turning pale.

I found I was walking slowly away from the danger-point. "I must go and tell Bickersteth," I excused myself. I passed the word down the dugout. Then I pulled myself together and got up to the front somehow. The men too were very panicky. Poor devils, they hadn't had a good sleep or a square meal for three days.

66

'Thud' went a bomb three bays up the trench. I licked my lips and felt for my revolver.

'Thud' went a bomb two bays away.

I was standing at our extreme right flank where we had posted a sentry two bays beyond the half-finished bomb-stop.

"Come along, let's get back to the bomb-stop," said I not very bravely. Just then round the traverse from the dugout came Serjeant Adams,[1] an old volunteer of many years' service in England. He was smoking a pipe and had a thin smile on his face.

"What's that, sir," he said pleasantly, "go back? No, sir, let's go forward," and he tucked his rifle under his arm and strolled along the trench alone—still smiling. A bomb burst in the bay beyond him. He climbed the traverse and took a snapshot with his rifle at some person beyond. A group of men stood wavering, and then I went and took my place beside him on the traverse.

Thirty or forty yards away I saw a hand and a grey sleeve come up out of the trench and throw a cylinder on the end of a wooden rod. It turned over and over in the air and seemed to take hours to approach. It fell just at the foot of the traverse where we stood, and burst with a shattering shock.

"The next one will get us," I thought.

Serjeant Adams pulled a bomb out of his pocket and threw it. I did the same, and immediately felt better. A young Lance-Corporal, Houghton, did the same. The next German bomb fell short. Then someone threw without remembering to pull the pin, and in a moment the bomb was caught up and thrown back at us by the enemy.

I snapped off my revolver once or twice at glimpses of the enemy. A little of last night's feeling was returning. Adams and Houghton were moving forward now, and I

[1] Serjeant Adams was given the Military Medal after this battle.

67

was watching them over the traverse, when I had the impression that someone was throwing stones. Suddenly I saw lying in the middle of the trench a small black object, about the shape and size of a large duck's egg. There was a red band round it and a tube fixed in one end of it. What could this be?

I guessed it must be some new sort of bomb.[1]

It was lying less than a yard from my foot; I was right in a corner of the trench. What was I to do? In an instant of time I thought: Had I the nerve to pick it up and throw it away? Should I step over it and run? Or stay where I was? There was no room to lie down. But too late. The bomb burst with a roar at my feet. My eyes and nose were full of dust and pungent fumes. Not knowing if I was wounded or not, I found myself stumbling down the trench with a group of groaning men. One of them was swearing and shouting in a high-pitched voice and bleeding in the leg. All the nerve was blasted out of us.

I fetched up almost in tears, shaken out of my senses, at Bickersteth's feet. My clothes were a little torn and my hand was bleeding, but that was all.

Bickersteth was very cool. He was watching the fight through a periscope and organising relays of bomb carriers.

"You must get these men together, Edmonds," he was saying, "and make a counter-attack."

"I'm damned if I will," said I; "I'm done for," and I lay and panted.

He looked at me and saw I was useless. I hadn't an ounce of grit left in me.

It was Wells who rallied the survivors and went up again to find my revolver, "shamefully cast away in the presence

[1] This is, I believe, the first recorded use in action of the German egg-bomb which could be thrown to a greater distance than their ordinary stick-bomb. It was, however, far less dangerous when it exploded.

of the enemy," and Serjeant Adams still holding his own.

"Come along, Edmonds," said Bickersteth, and in a minute or two I felt better and went up. We got the Lewis-gun out and the whole party moved forward. Houghton was throwing well. We rushed a bay, and Houghton, who was leading, found himself face to face with a German unter-offizier, the length of the next bay between them. He threw a lucky bomb which burst right in the German's face.[1] Their leader fallen, the heart went out of the enemy's attack. At the same moment there were two diversions. An 8-inch shell, one of those which had been falling occasionally on our right, suddenly landed right in the bay behind the German bomber, and his supporters fled. So ended their attack. But as we moved forward a sniper fired almost from behind us. I felt the bullet crack in my ear, and Corporal Matthews, who was walking beside me, preoccupied and intent, fell dead in the twinkling of an eye. I was looking straight at him as the bullet struck him and was profoundly affected by the remembrance of his face, though at the time I hardly thought of it. He was alive, and then he was dead, and there was nothing human left in him. He fell with a neat round hole in his forehead and the back of his head blown out.

Other big shells followed the first, so we decided not to hold that part of the trench. We propped up the dead Boche as a warning to his friends against the furthest traverse, and set to work on a better bomb-stop behind, just where Corporal Matthews was hit.

[1] I don't know how a Mills bomb could do this, but I saw it happen. Lance-Corporal Houghton knew nothing of the technique of bombing, and failed in the simple bomb-throwing tests out of the line. He probably let the lever fly, out of ignorance, and held the bomb. He received the Military Medal after this battle and was killed in our next.

It was now clear that we must set a definite limit to our fortress and make a strong bomb-stop on this most dangerous flank. The casual shelling seemed to have settled down into a regular slow bombardment of our extreme right with 8-inch shells, which fell at two-minute intervals just where we had killed the German N.C.O. Bickersteth decided to abandon the right-hand bay, even though it had a good dug-out, and to concentrate on the three bays below my earliest limit. Where I had set Griffin to work on a bomb-stop, he set about a larger and sounder plan. We must level one traverse flat and have a field of fire longer than the range of the German stick-bomb. He organised the work and left me in charge. We started to dig away the ten-foot cube of clay constituting the traverse by which Corporal Matthews had been shot. Almost as we approached and cut into it with pickaxes, the same sniper fired again from the village on our left, and a man called Pratt dropped like a stone just where the corporal had fallen. He, too, had a small round hole in his temple and the back of his skull blown away.

No one seemed very anxious to take his place on the bomb-stop. The body was moved down the trench and we stood around cutting gingerly into the pile of earth. I myself stood opposite the parapet gap through which the sniper fired and took care not to expose myself too much. We seemed to do very little good.

"Aw, give me that pick! Let me get at it!" suddenly roared one man, and he sprang up the traverse all exposed, striking giant blows that loosened the top of the mound where no one had dared to work. It was Jimmy Mills, and his time was short: for fifteen seconds, perhaps, he panted and drove his pick mightily, loosening the stiff clay, before the sniper fired again. Mills flung wide his pick and collapsed with a loud cry, inarticulate with rage and pain. The bullet had struck him in the left hip and pierced his bowels from side to side, emerging from the right.

"That's a third man dead," thought I. There were now two men dying on the trench floor, Pratt beating with helpless hands on the earth, the blood gushing from his nostrils, and now Mills, the old soldier, conscious and groaning, his trousers soaked with blood, thrilled with agony by every touch, by every movement. The other men, wounded earlier in the counter-attack, had been taken down into the dugout. These two more I brought to die in comfort in the deep safe fire-bay above it. Pratt was beyond hope. Hit in the same place as Corporal Matthews, his head was shattered: spatterings of brain lay in the pool of blood under him; but, though he had never been conscious since the shot was fired, he refused to die. An old Corporal looked after him, held his body and arms, which writhed and fought feebly as he lay. It was over two hours before he died, hours of July sunshine in a crowded space where perhaps a dozen men sat in a ditch ten yards long and five feet wide, reeking with the smell of blood, while all the time, above the soothing voice of the corporal, a gurgling and a moaning came from his lips, now high and liquid, now low and dry—a 'death-rattle' fit for the most bloodthirsty of novelists.

Old Mills, tough, bronzed, ginger-moustached and forty-one years old, lay beside this text "that taught the rustic moralist to die." No stretcher-bearers had come on with my wild adventure last night, but the old soldiers thought it best to leave him roughly bandaged until the inward wounds should close. Then he might have a chance. He was little, but hardened by fourteen years' soldiering and two previous wars. His work had not been in vain. The men at the traverse would be fully occupied in digging

71

away the soil which he had loosened, till, dusk, when someone could climb on top again.

The day wore on. No more Germans came, but squalls of shrapnel swept the valley behind us, and bombs thudded in the rear where we thought A company should be. I got some sleep in the afternoon. There was no bunk empty, but I flung myself on a stretcher by the side of Lee, my fellow-explorer of last night, and rested democratically.

That evening I began to understand our predicament. We had no good map, but Bickersteth made our situation clear. The village of Ovillers had been twice attacked from in front and twice successfully defended by the Prussian Guard. Further to the south at La Boisselle the British had advanced and driven the Germans back, which made it possible to take Ovillers in the flank. We had done more than this. We had advanced and placed ourselves in a trench behind the German stronghold, cutting it off from support and almost surrounding it; but at the same time we had now isolated ourselves, with Germans in front of us and behind us, the garrison of Ovillers in front, and those who were trying to relieve it behind. Consequently we were exposed to fire from almost any direction. On the other hand, to look for help we must turn back across the 1,000 yards of rough grass, impassable by day, which we had rushed across by night. This was actually looking for help in the direction of Germany. Bickersteth surprised me with the news that the heavy gun which persistently dropped shells near our right flank was an English gun, ignorantly trying to protect us, not a German gun ignorantly trying to destroy us. We had to be thankful for this protective fire, though the shell-splinters fell unpleasantly close. Since I had advanced too far in the night attack I had run into our own artillery fire, and the gunners still did not know exactly where we were.

We had little more cause for worry that day. The long silence came to Pratt at last; Mills, game and grumbling, got a little maudlin and was less in pain. We all began to suffer from thirst. Our water bottles, of course, had been filled at starting; but fighting is dry work. It was a muggy day and fear parches the throat. Most of us managed to hoard a few drops of water in case the ration-parties should not reach us early in the night. Work went on well at the bomb-stop, but the thousand cubic feet of clay were not easy to move. Before dark the Lewis-gun mounted on the next traverse could see at least the head and shoulders of a man two bays away. But now I found that the gun team had dispersed and only Bailey and Robinson, two good gunners, were with us. Bailey, who eventually became a serjeant, was a pale, square-jawed boy, whose firm mouth had impressed me as he stood to his gun during the attack. I always preferred the steadiness of the man who was afraid and yet carried on, to the lack of perspicacity that was the secret of most "brave" men's firmness. "Granny" Robinson, was a thin, spectacled young man, a very devoted husband with the manners of a gentleman. He was a Salvationist and the only "pious" soldier I ever met. Two of the best men in the trench, these two manned the gun in turn.

Nerves were tense that evening. The slight bomb casualties had one end of the dugout, where they lay uneasily under charge of a man whom we made a stretcher-bearer for the day; and good work he did. It always recurs to me that as we sat in the dugout, the wounded stirring uneasily, the officers feigning stolidity, a mat of men sleeping thick on bunks and floor, in the dusk of this rat-hole, one of the N.C.O.s, a loud-mouthed Sam Weller in khaki, broke into song with a Latin hymn to the Virgin, while the dugout listened in astonished silence.

With dusk came a renewal of activities. We arranged

73

reliefs from the dugout and put new life into the work on the bomb-stop. But a shower of rain, darkness, the flash of explosions before and behind, and the uncertainty of night, made strained nerves even less reliable. There was a disposition to panic. Every time I dozed off, when I was below, I was roused in a few moments by the hoarse staccato whisper down the shaft:

"Stand to! They're coming!"

No need to ask who was coming. Up the steps we ran, heart in mouth and weapons in hand, time after time, to find that a sentry had mistaken bursting shells for another bombing attack, or that a party of men was approaching from the other companies, for under the cloak of darkness we had regained touch with the world.

"Stand to, sir, they're coming!"

No! This time it is a thrice welcome ration party, with jars of rum and bully and biscuit for to-morrow.

"But water?" we ask, "where is the water, man?"

"Coming, sir, the serjeant-major is bringing it, and bombs and ammunition."

So to sleep again.

"Stand to! They're coming!"

Again I fling myself up the shaft, for it is death to be trapped in the cellars by an enemy with bombs on the surface.

"Who the hell are you?" the sentry gasps, his finger on the trigger, and his aim on an approaching shadow.

"All right, my man," says the Colonel's well-known voice, low and firm, but a little petulant.

"Hullo! There's Edmonds! How are you getting on?"

"Not so badly, sir, but I'd give my next leave for a whisky and soda."

"Done!" says the Colonel, groping in his side pocket,

74

and producing a Perrier bottle which he hands to me. "Your next leave is mine, Edmonds."

He had taken the precaution to bring a pint of that mixture with him over the top. The little joke and the spirits restore my nerve and I feel ten times more confident that the Colonel should merely be in the trench with us.

"They've had a bad time back there," he tells me.

It had not occurred to me that any but we had had bad, let alone worse, times.

"Suckling's gone, and Mayhew too, I'm afraid. They've been bombing all day." He doesn't mention that he, the Colonel, has been in the thick of it where Colonels have no business to be.

"How's Evers, sir?" I burst in.

"I think he's killed too," says the Colonel absently. "A company have no trench at all: it's all destroyed. I've withdrawn most of them, and the 16th are relieving them to-night."

"What about us, sir? Will they relieve us?"

"I don't think they'll be able to come up tonight. But you're all right here. This is a good trench—good dugouts. I wish I'd stayed here last night."

Presently comes the panic-stricken whisper again.

"Stand to! Stand to! They're coming again!"

"What is it? What is it?" asks the Colonel. "Damn them! They're all alike. Half-gotten weaklings. What's this panic about?" He gives orders. "This nonsense must stop. We must have some sleep down here. Edmonds, don't let them disturb me and Captain Bickersteth. Oh Lord, what's this?" Unknowingly in the dark he has stepped on Mills, who gives a loud groan.

"Wounded man, sir," say I, "name's Mills."

"Well, get him out of the way, Edmonds. Are you badly hurt, Mills? I'm sorry, but they shouldn't have put you here."

"Oh, it's awright, sir. I'm done for. Fourteen years' soldierin' and they got me this time. Wasn't you as hurt me, sir. Back seems all numb, sir. Can't get warm." He maunders on as the Colonel moves away.

"Put a stout fellah on the top here as sentry, and then get some sleep yourself."

I can never reproduce on paper all that it meant to me to have the Colonel with us in the trench. He was my hero. I admired his clothes and his horsemanship and his incisive speech and the adventures he had had in Africa, and his masterly way of handling troublesome superior officers; and I would yet think as highly of him again when I heard of his doings a few hours previously in the next trench, when the Germans attacked C company with bombs and all the officers were hit. Bickersteth had been as steady as a rock when I gave way; his calmness had held the trench, but now things were different. Now Cæsar had snatched up a shield and stood in the ranks of the Tenth Legion. Now the Little Corporal stood to a gun on the bridge of Arcola. Calm was restored and we had no more alarms. The night of terror ended soon, but the cry, "Stand to! They're coming!" and the stumbling climb in the darkness have not ceased to haunt my dreams.

No relieving company came that night, and at dawn we resigned ourselves to another day of misery and probably heavier attacks. I caught myself at one moment even discussing with a serjeant whether we could hold out against an "over the top" attack, and whether we should be justified even in surrendering if a large force rushed us, but that thought I managed to suppress.

We were certainly beginning to suffer badly from thirst. No water party ever arrived. The night before when I had gone to the corpses to take their water-bottles for the wounded, I had found that someone else had forestalled me and emptied them. Thirty-six hours ago we had each started with a quart in our bottles, but we had never expected to be left so long. Those men whose water was only finished this morning felt that they had been sufficiently cautious. Well, it was daylight now, and no considerable help could be expected till the darkness came again.

There were plenty of small things to be done. We were still struggling to move the mountain of traverse and had made such progress that we felt tolerably secure. I found a kind of repeating German rifle which the Colonel mounted in reserve to the Lewis-gun on the bomb-stop. Then the dugout sentry, looking over the top, saw Germans moving in a trench on the skyline near the sniper's post. We decided to watch them and not fire, to the Colonel's disgust when we reported. It seemed to be a relief moving away towards Thiepval. Then again further to the left I saw a man with a white flag standing and signalling in Morse code from a hedge near the entrance to the village. We saved this man from being shot by zealots and found a signaller of sorts who read the message, while I wrote it down. But nothing could be done with it; there only came a code[1] word of some kind repeated again and again, an arrangement of letters meaningless in any language we knew. I wandered up the trench and noticed Eliot, the boy who had wanted to stay behind. He was sitting on the fire-step joking with his neighbour, with his fears forgotten. He agreed with me that things weren't so bad, after all.

Presently an aeroplane flew low over us and we waved, hoping to give him our exact position, for the shells were still falling too close on our right. I conceived the mad plan of heliographing to him with a periscope mirror, a plan which hardly succeeded. Yet though the shells were falling so close to us that, an old Lancashire man, was hit

[1] Isetmhseetsee isaetie ngend.

in the leg by a spent splinter, of which he took no notice, continuing to sing lugubriously:

> " 'A love the ladies,
> 'A love to be among the girls";

and though at one time we abandoned the farthest sentry-post beyond the bomb-stop, during the course of the day the shelling slackened and ceased. We learnt afterwards that Cockburn, the Signalling officer, had seen the Germans massing to counter-attack our flank and had rung through to a battery ordering fire on his own responsibility and turned the scale in our bombing fight. Later from his observation post he had seen another counter-attack assembling and brought the artillery to disperse them before they had approached us. It was his barrage that had kept us safe, even if it was itself a slight danger.

I spent some time walking about the trench talking to different men. They were thirsty and tired but in wonderful spirits and ready for another fight. We improved the trench and rigged up a latrine in one corner of a bay. I brought out my reserve packet of De Reszkes and passed them round, duly receiving gratitude, though Woodbines would have been more popular. Some men grumbled at there being no rum ration, but we had decided that it would increase thirst.

Stanley, my servant, drew me into conversation out beyond our right flank now that the shelling had lifted and it was safe to explore that end of the trench. We looked at the dead "unteroffizer" and into the shaft of the abandoned dugout, of which I was rather frightened, for one shaft of it rose in another trench which joined ours farther along. He told me that he had been inside the dugout when yesterday's counter-attack began, and had run up the shaft, heavy-eyed, to find a huge Boche towering over him with upraised bomb. I asked him what he did. Stanley replied:

"I put my skates on." Probably the Boche did likewise.

Reader, before you condemn Stanley as a coward (for he was one of the bravest men I have known) reflect what you would do, if half-awake and half-asleep you were confronted with a man twice your size and a weapon that could blow seven men like you to rags in an instant. When two enemies meet in war, each surprising the other, they generally both dodge back into cover and devise a plan.

But Stanley soon came to the point. Furtively he produced a water-bottle, nearly half-full, and thrust it into my hands.

"Take it, sir," he said. "I've saved all this. I had plenty."

"Stanley, you're a sportsman, but I can't take it off you. I've drunk up all my own."

"You'd better have it, sir."

"If you're sure you can spare some, give it to the wounded. They're wanting it pretty badly."

He did so, but looked disappointed about it.

Water for the wounded was getting a serious problem, so we decided to send a message. A man volunteered at once to take it over the top. Lance-Corporal Vinter went to show him the way out of the trench, but the man had hardly got clear when he was shot dead. In a few minutes Vinter and Corporal Goodbody came to me and offered to try again. They went out carefully and dashed over the bank safely to the trench in the rear, where the 16th had taken the place of A company. Only a bottle or two of water could be spared, for the present.

It was another muggy grey day, and steadily growing drier and thirstier.

A buzz of excitement down on the left brought me there again to find the sentry and others exposing themselves over the parapet. They could see Germans surrendering —hundreds of them—to somebody on our left. Later we

79

learnt they were the last 120 men of the garrison of Ovillers, the 3rd Prussian Guard, the "Cockchafers," two days cut off from supplies by us who were planted in their rear. The others had retired towards Mouquet Farm and Thiepval through the trench where we had seen them on the skyline.

The success of Corporal Vinter and the combined effects of thirst and boredom produced several volunteers to go and fetch water. Bickersteth would not let me go. A tall, thin, raw-boned man made the next trip, with a tactical report from the Colonel. This runner came back safe and panting, and inspired several more. But water was scarce in the trench behind as well as in ours.

Towards noon, old Mills, lying on the firestep, groaning only when jolted unavoidably in the narrow way, began to give up hope. He thought he was dying and turned sentimental. Plucking feebly at my arm as I passed, he tried to give me his blessing. I was a fine young gentleman, and had always been a good officer to him, and if it hadn't been for me they would have all been done for. I was most embarrassed and only with difficulty told him not to talk like that, for he was good for another fourteen years' soldiering. Neither of us believed what I was saying.[1] I quieted him at last with a dash of brandy from my flask, for which the doctor cursed me handsomely later, for it might have killed him instead of sending him to sleep. One of the wounded men below lost his nerve a little and moaned for water, till we thought we had better send another volunteer. A man whom I had always thought unsociable, offered to go. He took several water-bottles and came back with enough for the wounded, making a second journey safely with a companion.

The wounded were now satisfied, but most of the trench

[1] But we were wrong. He made a rapid recovery.

80

licked their dry lips and prayed for nightfall, still many hours away. It was specially aggravating to possess those two jars of useless rum, all of which we would have willingly exchanged for half a gallon of water.

Looking up from the dugout mouth in the sullen dry mid-afternoon, I suddenly saw a stranger strolling over the top towards us, though we had no volunteers at work just then. Soon I saw the 16th badge on his arm.

"Come down!" said I, "jump to it! They're sniping like the devil across here!"

"I'm all right, sir," said he, looking round casually enough, and indeed no shot had been fired at him.

"What have you come for?"

"Captain Moore sent me to find out where you were."

"Well, you're the first man who's come over without being fired at. Come down the dugout. The Colonel will see you."

He sat on the dugout steps and told the Colonel what he knew, which was not much. We gave him some rum and sent him back with a message reporting more movement in that skyline trench.

The Colonel had been feeling uneasy all day about the situation, thinking that we were not controlling our own destinies enough. We looked over the tactical position. On the right I showed him the dugout which opened into the other trench. Flaring up with interest at once, he began to threaten me with all kinds of horrors, fighting patrols, general advances till we met resistance, extensions of the position to the right. It seemed to me that we had already bitten off as much as we could chew, but inaction never suited him. Before long I found myself under orders, with Corporal Houghton and any men I wanted, to explore the loop trench leading round the dugout. If we met no enemy we should have plenty of fun with our own barrage. Pleased to be singled out for the Colonel's confidence, and

81

chosen without question before Wells, who had all along been in the background, I hardly remembered to be afraid. So the Corporal and I decided to start alone and work round from the left.

Corporal Houghton stripped off his equipment, put a bomb in each pocket and stood ready with another in his hand. I drew my revolver and felt confident again, finding moral support in being the chosen one again, to stand in the limelight at the post of danger. I slid gently over the shoulder-high bomb-stop on the left, keeping low to escape our old friend, the sniper. The corporal following, I crept along the trench. One bay we had to pass, and one ruined traverse, till where the trench faded out of existence among the shell-holes the switch trench should turn off to the right. The parapet was low and made me stoop. I went stealthily round the traverse and poked the muzzle of my revolver into the meditations of a British subaltern who was sitting quietly on the fire-step playing with the pin of a bomb.

"Good Lord!" I said, leaning against the traverse. I saw by his badges he was of the 16th. "How did you get here?"

"All the battalion's here. Boches have evacuated the village. Our men are right ahead there, look!"

Now I could see men in khaki moving across the low ground on the left and the figures in the skyline trench were now revealed as Englishmen too.

"Have you got any water?" said I.

"Sure." He gave up his water-bottle, which we emptied in a moment. "There's a party coming through with water in a minute."

Before long we were back at the dugout explaining to the Colonel. The subaltern of the 16th, a swarthy young man, rather supercilious and sceptical of our heroisms, was followed by a group of Tommies bringing petrol tins full of water, which we swallowed in huge draughts. It tasted of petrol, but it was damp and cool. After half a pint from the subaltern's bottle, I drank at least a quart from the can, and was thirsty again in a moment. The joy of relief had lifted any fear of present danger, and we all drank and talked and drank again. Everyone was happy but poor old Mills, who was still prevented from disturbing his stomach with more than a little water.

The grassy slope about the village was covered with men. A bombing party pressed on beyond our defences to the right, for the barrage had lifted. Other parties were mopping up the area behind and on the left. One group under Colonel Cornwall, newly commanding his battalion, after bombing and surrounding an enemy post right in our rear in the valley, came on and established their head-quarters in our trench. Colonel Cornwall came up and greeted me with the enthusiasm of a boy who meets a friend at a very exciting football match.

We all found ourselves standing about carelessly on the top, for the snipers were cleared off the Ovillers Crest and we were only visible from the Pozières Ridge far away to the right—not that we cared if we were visible from Berlin. But Pozières was developing troubles of its own. The Australians were going in the line there to attack it, and as we stood and talked, the skyline heaved and smoked, throwing up fountains and jets of soil and grey smoke as if it were a dark grey sea breaking heavily on a reef. The bombardment grew thicker and thicker: clouds of smoke sprang up and drifted across its torn groups of trees; the spurts of high explosive rose close together, till it seemed that the very contour of the hill must be changed.

Our thoughts were recalled two miles by the loud crash of shrapnel almost overhead. A "mad minute" of shells rained from the air and burst above Ovillers. The shrapnel banged like dinner gongs dropped downstairs, and a black pall hung along the ridge. Like so many German shells, they burst too high, and their line of fire threw the danger-zone on to the village two hundred yards away.

As we had now been relieved Bickersteth was keen to get the company away as soon as possible, back to camp on the Albert Road where we had left our packs. The wounded were to be left in charge of the 16th Battalion; we should have a big enough job getting ourselves down the line. I tried to get permission to leave the Lewis-gun ammunition, which had given such trouble in moving forward, as the 16th would have been glad of it, but Bickersteth was most definite; it must be brought, for we were not going right out of the line and should want it again in a day or two. Before we left we buried our dead men in a shell-hole in front of the trench. We made rough wooden crosses to mark the graves, but no one seemed inclined to say a prayer. I was much too shy to suggest it, being only an officer, while the burial was carried out by the friends of the dead men.

§ 6

About half-past six Bickersteth led off the long procession in single file down the trench. I brought up the rear and picked up our second Lewis-gun, which had never been with us, but had taken up a position of its own near the cross-roads. Collecting this party we lost touch at once with the company, but the six of us followed on, loaded down with the gun and those accursed magazine buckets. Instead of going back across the valley Bickersteth had led the way direct towards Ovillers into a maze of German trenches at the entrance to the village. We pursued him, with the help of ignorant passers-by. We passed a bomb dump with cases of stick-bombs and egg-bombs, and another kind more like our Mills bombs, but fired by the pulling of a loop (these I never saw in use); then passed a series of doorways leading into a large dugout system which I did not then know was the famous trench Dressing-station of Ovillers, capable of holding three hundred lying cases, but lately used as a mortuary and impenetrable. Presently I saw a likely trench cutting across the valley, and having no news of Bickersteth, decided to risk it. I went on in front of the party to pick the way. There was mud in the bottom, though the sides were white chalk, and a few corpses at that repulsive stage when the skin turns slimy black, so I followed the example of the men, climbing out and following the parapet.

It was then, turning back, that I knew what the novelists mean by a "stricken field." The western and southern slopes of the village had been comparatively little shelled; that is, a little grass had still room to grow between the shell-holes. The village was guarded by tangle after tangle of rusty barbed wire in irregular lines. Among the wire lay rows of khaki figures, as they had fallen to the machine-guns on the crest, thick as the sleepers in the Green Park on a summer Sunday evening. The simile leapt to my mind at once of flies on a fly paper. I did not know then that twice in the fortnight before our flank attack, had a division been hurled at that wire-encircled hill, and twice had it withered away before the hidden machine-guns. The flies were buzzing obscenely over the damp earth; morbid scarlet poppies grew scantily along the white chalk mounds; the air was tainted with rank explosives and the sickly stench of corruption.

We hurried on. As we approached the embanked side of the great road, three or four heavy shells, 8-inch at least, came over and burst at hundred-yard intervals along it. Retaliation was beginning for the continuous punishment of Pozières.

"Come on!" I shouted. "Let's get a move on. This is a bad place to be caught in." I hurried on under a culvert and out again up the next spur. But the men could carry no more. Worn out when they started, overloaded with these awkward buckets, they could make no better pace through mud and shell-holes and up this rough slope. When we reached the top of the hill, there was no mistake about it. The Germans were barraging the crest with heavies and probably would counter-attack. Here I lost my temper. It was a case of getting my men through or saving this wretched ammunition. We were three-quarters of a mile from the front line. The stuff was safe. I decided to disobey orders. Two gunner officers were watching the artillery duel close by. I set the men to work dumping the stores in a convenient shell-hole and ran back to the gunners. In great haste I committed to their charge one Lewis-gun and I forget how many magazines. One of them was, I believe, a colonel, and looked surprised, but I waited for nothing, and fled, shouting to my men to run down the trench till they got out of the barrage. All this last you must imagine amongst the crash and roar of bursting shells, several within a few yards of us. We ran like hell, myself last! Then came an incident which has often given me doubts where my duty lay. Of course my own men had the first call on me; of course when retreating I was right in bringing up the rear. But as I fled I noticed a signaller with head-phones on in a "cubby-hole" dug into the trench-wall. I pulled up short and shouted to him through the thunders, asking where we were, and if the company had passed that way. He made no answer, but slowly raised his head and looked at me with blank appealing eyes. I saw that two rivulets of blood were running slowly from his throat into the collar of his tunic.

Now what was the motive of my action I cannot say. Irritated at receiving no answer, horrified at the unexpected, feeling that I could do no good and that a signaller could not be far from reliefs, I shouted vaguely that I would send him help and ran on after my men. A hundred yards further down the trench and round a bend, I passed a large party from our C company, sheltering from the bombardment in another row of "cubby-holes." I only lingered to tell their stretcher-bearers of the bleeding signaller, and rushed on till I caught up my own men. Whether he bled to death before they found him, or whether perhaps he was only scratched and dazed, I never knew: but his face remained with me.

We were through the barrage and my men had halted outside a dugout and were drinking with some charitable riflemen. We were as thirsty again as if we had drunk nothing since yesterday, and emptied all the petrol cans of water they could spare. Then on again down the trench, lighter for the loss of the ammunition, but dog-tired and footsore. We were well below the skyline and a mile or more from the nearest section of the front when we encountered a large party of men from a strange division, without an officer. They were carrying water up the line, unarmed. A stretcher-party converged on us, and fifty yards of trench was jammed with about a hundred men going different ways. Suddenly the shelling broke out again, but not within a furlong of us. It was near enough for some overstrained stretcher-bearer. In a hysterical voice he suddenly shouted.

"Aw! Look! They're comin' over the top!"

In an instant the trench was in confusion. My little band of stalwarts was swept away by a rush of panic-stricken stretcher-bearers. Shouting and trampling, the whole hundred men ran in all directions. It was an amazing example of the madness of an uncontrolled mob. My serjeant was carried right down the trench out of sight. I was rushed a few paces along it, shouting that we were a mile from the enemy. When I looked back I saw to my joy, absurd though it was, my six men, who following me in single file had been clear of the crowd, lying up on the parapet loading their rifles and looking for an aim at imaginary foes. The water-carriers vanished utterly; where they ran to I don't know; but at least we had got still another drink from them.

We assembled and trudged on again, round traverse after traverse, over innumerable obstacles, for the most part through deserts of chalk and wire and sand-bags, but sometimes meeting troglodytes who gave us water, always more petrol-tainted water, and directed us down the line. Once we came into a sort of quarry with dugouts in it and the broken-down ambulance wagon of which Richardson had spoken, and then on again through endless windings of battered trenches.

At last we came out into an open valley in the dusk and moved across turf again, but it was turf scored by the hoofs of many mules and worn into ruts by wagon-wheels. Everywhere columns of transport with the night's supplies of food and ammunition were moving up, and batteries were changing position. One had just had a horse killed, had cut it loose and left it there by the track. Asking our way we drifted over a low hill and stumbled somehow into the lines of bivouacs that flanked the road outside Albert. More by luck than by judgment we reached our own officers' lines, to find we had been given up for lost.

They met me as one returned from the dead, where the company messes were dining by candlelight off the ground. I was the hero of the moment; but my glory faded when Bickersteth asked after the Lewis-gun and I told him that it had been abandoned in a shell-hole that could not locate on the map. But on the whole we were well received. Two hundred yards from our camp was a six-inch naval gun which fired every few minutes over our heads, not only jarring our nerves but extinguishing every light in the camp at every blast. We slept that night in a closed-in gun-emplacement of earth and hurdles, happily except that Richardson found a snake in his bed.

Casualties to the battalion in this battle:

Killed	...	3 officers,	45 other ranks.
Wounded	...	5 officers,	76 other ranks.
Total	...	8	121

One hundred and twenty-nine: that is about a quarter of those who took part in the battle, a small proportion considering the rashness of the enterprise.

[British Official Communiqué—July 17th, 1916, 2.15 p.m.—gave this report: "On our left flank in Ovillers-la-Boisselle where there has been continuous hand to hand fighting since July 7th, we captured the remaining strongholds of the enemy together with 2 officers and 124 guardsmen who formed the remnants of its brave garrison. The whole village is now in our hands."]

CHAPTER III

THE MIDDLE YEAR OF THE WAR, 1916-1917

§ 1

WAR is a contest of nerves. That army wins which in times of tribulation can longest bear the mental strain of plague, pestilence and famine; battle, murder and sudden death. In the middle years of the Great War the strain began to tell. Early in 1916 all the European armies were tuned to the highest pitch of mind and body; late in 1917 all were perilously near the breaking point. In 1916 English, French and Germans alike saw victory within their grasp, and expected it after every local advantage; in 1917 the war seemed likely to go on for ever, and victory had receded into a visionary distance. The weakest links in the chain began to give: Russia collapsed; Italy went down but recovered; even France, after bearing the burden and heat of the day, showed signs of weakening: for a time the war was sustained by England and Germany alone: England striking desperate blows, with failing courage, Germany stubbornly resisting without hope. At this moment there was no question of sudden victory, only of prolonging the war until one or other should give up the contest. As yet no one understood that the American armies might turn the scale.

The Somme battle raised the morale of the British Army. Although we did not win a decisive victory, there was what matters most in war, a definite and growing sense of superiority over the enemy, man to man. The attacks in mid-July were more successful and better managed than those of July 1st. In August and September things went better still. When the tanks made their surprising appearance on September 15th rejoicing knew no bounds; but the Germans were not yet badly beaten enough nor our skill great enough for us to make the best use of our winnings, and the autumn rains rendering further movement impossible brought us to a standstill in the mud. My regiment had by no means completed its task at Ovillers. A week after the battle described we went up again to Pozières to carry out a large bombing attack on the left flank of the Australians and lost another fifty men before going out for a fortnight's rest thirty miles away near Abbeville. One of the most cold-blooded processes of war is fattening for the slaughter. Twice already we had gone into the Battle of the Somme to make food for powder, and now a second time were withdrawn for rest and training, and to be made "up to strength" by drafts of new recruits sent out from England. A disbanded battalion of cyclists from East Anglia gave us one of the best drafts we ever received, sufficient in numbers for us to be able to undertake a third tour in the battle late in August. Near Thiepval the brigade went over the top behind a "creeping barrage" of shrapnel, a device newly invented, which threw into our hands a strong German trench redoubt with two hundred and fifty prisoners—one of the neatest battles of the war, and one highly commended by the authorities above, even by our masters, the Daily Papers. In this affair Bickersteth and the company behaved brilliantly. I did nothing, being in reserve until the next day, when under his orders I carried out a small bombing

attack against an outlying German trench, which just en-
abled me to claim a share in the battle. For some days
more we held Skyline Trench, a waste of shell-holes always under fire, where the shape of the ground suffered
continual change from the effects of bombardment, and
one always lost one's way. Then my regiment's part in the
Battle of the Somme was over; but I had another alle-
giance to consider. To my family; to my parents living
abroad, to my brothers and sisters in France and else-
where, the Somme battle came to have a different meaning
when in October one of my brothers was killed.

We spent most of the autumn out in rest, marching and
drilling among familiar villages, enlivened by alarums and
excursions towards the battle-field. Having got through
three of the worst phases of the "Great Push" with credit
and without disaster, we gave ourselves airs as veteran soldiers. There was a regrettable tendency to "buck" about
one's battles all day long, to swap experiences with other
soldiers and to "tell the tale" to newcomers. We were quite
sure that we had got the Germans beat: next spring we
would deliver the knock-out blow. Much was to be endured
before that day should come. In November the division
was sent up again to the Somme to a point pushed far
forward into the German lines. Stumbling across miles
of old battlefield, first through horse-lines and dumps, then
through lines of guns concealed in mud-holes, then through
dreary wastes of clay pitted with shell-holes full of mud,
strewn with a litter of old equipment and shell-splinters,
and smelling vilely of six-months' old corpses, one came
to a wide swampy valley commanded on this side by the
Pozières ridge which we held, and on the other by Lou-
part Wood which screened the German guns and the distant towers of Bapaume. Down in the bottom, in the cen-
tral middle distance, there rose out of the mud a strange
conical mound of white chalk, a hundred feet high. What

Gallic chieftain slain by Cæsar in the land of the Ambiani lay beneath this tumulus we cared not. It was known as the Butte of Warlencourt (which we pronounced exactly as in English) and marked the German front line. While the artillery of the two armies lay back on the hill-tops strafing anyone who moved by day down the long slopes to the Butte, the infantry crouched and hid in the mud of the valley bottom. Even by night one could scarcely move, for the enemy spasmodically plastered with shell-fire every line of approach. To go or come from the line was a nightmare adventure and, once there, one dared not move for fear of the enemy machine-guns on the Butte of Warlencourt. That ghastly hill, never free from the smoke of bursting shells, became fabulous. It shone white in the night and seemed to leer at you like an ogre in a fairy tale. It loomed up unexpectedly, peering into trenches where you thought yourself safe: it haunted your dreams. Twenty-four hours in the trenches before the Butte finished a man off. In the severe winter[1] that was setting in, no precautions could prevent men going sick from frostbite and fevers; and no one was in good health. The worst disease of that winter was "Trench feet" a sort of foot-rot caused by standing with one's feet continually wet and cold. At best it was extremely painful, and at worst it required the amputation of the patient's feet.

In these wretched surroundings we found one solace. We used to sit in the dugout and sing; music-hall songs and folk-songs, and the ribald old army songs which have been handed down by ten generations of soldiers from mouth to mouth. Being young and strong, I stood the physical conditions pretty well, and generally recovered from the effects of trench life after a night's sleep. On the other hand, the shell-fire began to tell on me. The terrors of

[1] Excepting 1928-29 the winter of 1916-17 was the coldest of this century.

battle added to the hardships of artic exploration were overwhelming, and after three tours in front of the Butte I was a nervous wreck. Nor, I suppose, was I alone in this, as one-third of the whole division went sick, and on their side of the line the Germans were in just the same plight.

We spent Christmas out in rest at Albert, a market town of some size still containing a few civilian inhabitants. This was a very happy time. My brother sent me the "Ghost Stories of an Antiquary" which frightened me so much that I shivered alone in my billet at night. I had now been a year at the front, and began to make up a diary of my experiences. It may be interesting to the reader to hear how a subaltern at the war had actually passed his time.

§ 2

ANALYSIS OF A DIARY KEPT AT THE FRONT DURING THE YEAR 1916

It is not easy to divide a year of war into so many days "up the line" and so many "down the line" because one was very often not quite one thing or the other. Actually in the front-line trench there were very few men at any given moment, because in war every unit tries to withdraw some small proportion of men into reserve. For example, an infantry division of 20,000 men holding a sector of the front might have two of its three brigades "up" and one in reserve. In the same way each forward brigade might have two of its four battalions "up" and two in reserve; and each of the two battalions would try to keep two of its four companies in reserve. This means that on the divisional

94

front of three or four miles, eight companies at a time might be sufficient to hold the front line, 1,000 men out of the 20,000 that made a division. The men kept in reserve by the battalion would probably be near enough to be continually under fire and on the alert. They would hardly dare to lay aside their arms, clothes or gas-masks, and in some trenches they led a more disturbed and dangerous life than the men in the front line. On the other hand, in quiet trenches they might enjoy a holiday punctuated only by occasional visits to the front line to help with the endless digging. To be in reserve, then, may mean being near the front in reserve to a battalion, or to a brigade and a little farther back, or to the division, which meant ease and safety. Finally, the whole division once or twice a year would be withdrawn from the line for rest and training.

I find that in the year 1916 I spent 65 days in the front-line trenches, and 36 more in supporting positions close at hand; that is, 101 days which may be described as under fire. In addition 120 days were spent in reserve positions near enough to the line to march up for the day when work or fighting demanded, and 73 days were spent out in rest. This leaves 72 days for various contingencies. Twenty-one days were spent at schools of instruction; 10 in hospital, with German measles, of all humiliating diseases for a soldier; 17 days on two short visits to England on leave (I got leave about once in six months throughout the war; a private soldier got much less); 9 days at the Base camp on my way to join the regiment; and the remaining 14 days in travelling from one of these places to another. On active service one is never long in one place but continually packing up and marching a few miles with apparent aimlessness, explained only by the intricate staff plans for concentrating troops where they will be required. In 1916 I packed up all my goods and moved about eighty times, of which fourteen were by train or bus and the rest on my own feet.

The 101 days under fire contain twelve "tours" in the trenches, varying in length from one to thirteen days. The battalion made sixteen in all during the year, but I missed two on leave, one in hospital and one "on a course"; all four being "cushy" tours. We were in action four times during my twelve tours in the trenches. Once I took part in a direct attack, twice in bombing actions, and once we held the front line from which other troops advanced. I also took part in an unsuccessful trench-raid. On six other occasions I had to go up the line either for working parties or to reconnoitre.

This must be a typical experience shared by many hundreds of thousands of infantrymen who spent a year continuously at the front during the middle period of the war.

§ 3

At the end of January 1917 the division moved south to take over trenches from the French on the banks of the river Somme, which wound through the battle line in sinuous curves. It is a sluggish swampy stream not unlike the Thames above Oxford, splitting into numerous channels which flow round osier beds and water meadows and market gardens, between low chalk downs. In war it forms a military obstacle impassable to troops except at rare bridges; and where it came diagonally through the trench lines it made a gap half a mile wide, of reed beds, marshy pools and willow clumps, inhabited only by flocks of water birds. Every morning at stand-to scores of wild duck rose off the marshes and flew to their daily feeding-grounds pursued by a rain of machine-gun bullets from both armies. Our position was on a hill-top looking down on the antique town of Péronne, which lay on the other bank of the Somme in German hands. Opposite to us, the very high hill of Mont St. Quentin was the watch-tower from which the enemy commanded all the country for many miles.

Where we went in the line the trenches were well made and the attentions of the enemy not too severe. All through February the ground was iron hard with frost, which saved us from mud, the least endurable element of warfare. But we were short-handed, which meant continual and strenuous working-parties; and the trenches were very close together—at their nearest point only about forty yards—which meant continuous close observation of their front line to guard against raids. In these trenches a young officer's life centred round the duty of patrolling No Man's Land. Every night one or other of the subalterns in a front-line company would have to harden his heart, select a stout companion from the ranks, and creep like the serpent, on his belly, over the parapet into the darkness. Moving inch by inch with the delicate four-footed tread of a toad stalking a fly, halting and lying frozen flat at every creak of the barbed wire or scamper of a trench rat, dragging his body through the mud, he would move forward a yard, five yards, twenty yards in half an hour. He must be still and silent, so still that tiny sounds came to him full of meaning out of the night, till he heard the stealthy coughing of the German sentries at their posts and their infinitely careful shuffling from foot to foot. He would lie on frozen mud, minute after aching minute, because shadowy figures were creeping along the German parapet twenty yards away, and the movement of a muscle would bring instant death. He would hear the steady thump, thump of his own beating heart. If the night was clouded he might well be lost in No Man's Land and hear human sounds seeming to come from all directions, uncertain which were German and which our own, until a landmark, some well-known tangle of rusted wire, or conformation of heaped earth above a shell-hole, set him right. Best of all on clear nights was the Pole Star, on his left hand going out, and on his right hand crawling home. This was a new aspect of nature, the aspect of a mouse cautiously emerging from its hole to make adventurous voyage five yards into a world of perils. At any moment, even if you escaped the obvious danger of being noticed or killed by a hostile post or patrol, some casual sentry might send up a Verey light to land by accident beside you, bringing immediate exposure; or low-bursting shrapnel from guns cutting the barbed wire might strike you where you lay; and this danger was as great from your own as from the German guns. Where No Man's Land was wider, larger operations of patrolling, like a game of poachers and gamekeepers, might be carried out, and once in No Man's Land you were safe from bombardment between the two fires. Not so where the trenches were close together.

The great frost of February 1917 thawed at last, bringing rain and mud and snow. This moment the Germans selected to retire twenty or thirty miles to the Hindenburg line, a newly dug trench system, leaving to us the shelled area of the Somme battle-field. As they retired they laid waste the country. To break down bridges, to blow up the cross-roads with mines, to drive off the cattle and burn the crops, was legal by the barbarous code of war. In just that way Wellington covered his retreat to the lines of Torres Vedras. In sheer malice to France they also looted the countryside, destroyed and defiled churches and ancient monuments, cut down the cider orchards on which the peasants lived, and carried away men, women and children into slavery. These are the things that make it hard for Frenchmen to forgive their enemies so quickly as we have done. From our hill-top on the Somme we saw the smoke of fifteen burning villages and the flames bursting from the historic church and library of Péronne, sights which moved us little. In war

> "Blood and destruction shall be so in use
> And dreadful objects so familiar."

that the mind turns rather to the chance of victory. How far would the Germans retire? Would this begin the victorious advance? Should we keep them "on the run"?

There was a period of open fighting. Squadrons of dragoons charged machine-gun posts, with uproarious infantry running behind. Advance-guards moved along open roads as they had been taught to do at Aldershot. Parties of scouts ranged boldly a mile ahead of their battalions, a very different trade from that of "belly-crawling" between the lines in fixed trench-warfare. The excitement maintained us through long days with insufficient food and nights without shelter in a naked land. There were ten several falls of snow in April 1917, and we often slept with no roof over our heads. Our advance ended in a night attack near Epéhy where we set out in the rain to destroy a German outpost in a wood. It grew pitch dark and the rain turned to sleet and then to heavy snow. We wandered in the dark, amid falling shells, and my horse died of exposure. In the morning we withdrew, unable to find a way through the German barbed wire, to reorganise; and when we advanced again they slipped away unseen to the Hindenburg line. After this we went back to rest. Six weeks in frozen trenches and another six of fighting in the open had been galling. Thanks to a very active and able general the division had done well and been highly praised by Haig himself, but what of the men? It was at this time that I examined myself and found that I was not the man I had been a year before. Though I had tried very conscientiously to do my duty in these actions, and had kept up appearances, fighting had entirely ceased to be good fun. No longer did I recount my adventures with gusto in long letters to my mother.

The sustaining force at this stage of the war was esprit de corps. It so happened that throughout the emergencies of the last nine months our company had been extremely lucky. The battalion itself had never been cut to pieces, which is surprising enough, but in the company it seemed to be always the newcomers who were killed. The old hands now mostly serjeants and corporals, survived everything. "Old soldiers never die; they simply fade away"; the army song seemed to give a true account of us. As for the officers, the colonel, the adjutant and Bickersteth were all promoted and transferred but for more than a year I had been second in command of B company, with occasional intervals in command, and B company was my joy and my salvation. All things were bearable if one bore them "with the lads." Battles would have become terrible beyond endurance, if pride did not make a man endure what his comrades endured. Who cared that Russia was deserting her allies? Who cared that politicians were betraying the soldiers? Here at the front was all the honour that could be found, in the year 1917 when honour was a name almost forgotten in the world.

It happened that fortune treated me lightly between May and September. We went into a cushy sector of the front and held outposts in open country a mile away from the Germans. No adventures came our way in the early summer, through which we sat and recuperated, looking across green fields to the barbed wire in front of the Hindenburg line, a dusty streak in the distance. Here a studious fit seized me and I sent home for a copy of Browning. At first I was mocked in the dugout as a high-brow for reading "The Ring and the Book," but saying nothing I waited until one of the scoffers idly picked it up. In ten minutes he was absorbed, and in three days we were fighting for turns to read it, and talking of nothing else at meals. I had three days' leave in Paris, then a long leave in England, and soon after that, was sent on a course of instruction. All France was full of training schools where officers came down from the trenches for a short holiday and intensive study of some military subject. This was an army school for budding company commanders. Glad as I was to be away from the battle, I hated being away from the company. They went into the Third Battle of Ypres in August and fought the first battalion "show" in which I had not taken part. I was bored and nervy and irritable, moping rather than enjoying my rest, arguing with the instructors instead of learning from them. It was a proud tradition of the war that a subaltern on the spree had to be a roystering blade, devoted to women and wine; and we did our best. But of all holidays in the war I made least of this one. I was hating the war and at the same time longing to be back with the regiment.

The second detailed narrative of a battle begins with my return to duty in September 1917.

CHAPTER IV

AN ADVENTURE IN THE THIRD BATTLE OF YPRES, KNOWN TO THE SOLDIERS AS THE BATTLE OF PASSCHENDAELE

§ 1

OUTWARDLY I have rarely enjoyed such a happy time as the autumn of 1917, and inwardly have rarely been more miserable. We spent long and gorgeous days in the sun, riding over the downs, lounging under the poplars that lined the high road, and training hard for the approaching battle. We were fit and numerous, well housed and well amused. This was in the undulating country near St. Omer, more than thirty miles from the battle; yet the doom that hung over the armies for so many years was now most dark and imminent. After a long period out of the trenches and a long leave in England I could not bring myself again to face the battlefield, but let my mind run riot with apprehensions and superstitions. Under the calm surface of our country life in this golden autumn weather, my mind (and, I suppose, not mine alone) was a turmoil of wild thoughts and fears from which the dreadful fancies of malingering, desertion, even suicide could not be altogether excluded. At this date, though one hardly realised it, the overstrain of war had ruptured the nerves of

Russia, shaken the balance of France and was about to bring Italy to disaster. Before the hopeless prospect of a struggle which seemed to offer no end but death now or death deferred, even the heart of an English lad grew sick: a lad who was senior subaltern of his battalion and just promoted to command a company.

Every scrap of news coming down from Passchendaele told of futile struggle with the swamps of the salient, of useless tanks bogged in the slime, of mismanaged partial attacks, of hopeless plans and angry generals, of great losses in men and small gains even in ground.

On a hot September night we marched to the railway, my horse shying all the way at its black shadow under the harvest moon. In the station yard I talked dismally with Thorburn, one of my subalterns, recently joined from another battalion which in the past had been less lucky than mine. We counted the chances and thought it time for this battalion to take a knock.

Before going up into the line the battalion spent three days in a camp between Poperinghe and Ypres. There were rows of tents standing on dry mud, with low walls of sandbags built up eighteen inches round each tent to protect sleeping men from the side-blast of the bombs which were dropped by German aeroplanes every night. One evening Thorburn and I went in to Poperinghe to dine at La Poupée, and were damnably bombed by a low-flying aeroplane as we "lorry-hopped" back along the Ypres road. Another day four of us, disguised in private soldiers' tunics, went up by day beyond St. Julien to reconnoitre the front and to lay out a tape on which the first wave of the battalion might form up before "jumping off." This was a terrifying day on which I was quite demoralised. Almost at the beginning we found ourselves walking along

Admiral's Road through a huge dump of ammunition which had been set on fire by enemy bombardment. Among the burning wooden boxes to left and right shells fizzled and burst alarmingly. At last we reached a square structure of concrete as large as a cottage, on the top of a slope, and learned that it was the captured German pillbox called Cheddar Villa. From here all the battlefield lay open; the long bare slope down to St. Julien; the valley of the Steenbeek, choked with wreckage, churned into swamp, and dotted with derelict tanks; the rising ground to Poelcapelle, and in the far distance fields and pastures new, green trees and a church spire. It brought back to me a memory of childhood, of the "Pilgrim's Progress" which I had not read since nursery days: here was Christian descending into the Valley of Humiliation and seeing in the distance the Delectable Mountains "beautified with woods, vineyards, fruits of all sorts, flowers, also with springs and fountains, very delectable to behold," but in the path there lay "a wilderness, a land of deserts and pits; a land of drought, and of the shadow of death!" There was "also in that valley a continual howling and yelling, as of people under unutterable misery, who there sat bound in afflictions and irons; over that valley hang the discouraging clouds of confusion; death also doth always spread his wings over it. In a word, it is every whit dreadful, being utterly without order"; while "at the other end of this valley lay blood, bones, ashes and mangled bodies of men, even of pilgrims that had gone this way formerly."

Our duty somehow done, we returned to camp at midnight. Next day I was miserable beyond belief, description or cure. A sort of insensible numbness, such as seems to envelop criminals in the condemned cell, settled on my spirits, suggesting to me in many ways which I rationally knew to be impossible that the Valley of the Shadow might be avoided. There was much routine work to be done, which I did in an unreal mood as if it were a game, a piece of play-acting. My true self had been filled with the pre-sentiment that this was the end, that I was marked to die or be crushed in the military machine; I thought the human spirit could endure no longer postponement of the terror. I arranged that day to meet my brother in another regiment, but we were too busy to see much of one an-other, and I too constrained to be very friendly. Before going up the line on the afternoon of October 3rd, we moved again to another camp under the walls of Ypres; and while the men had tea I went to Brigade Headquarters, where at a company commanders' meeting we checked and explained to one another the details of our plans. By this time I was beside myself and noticed how one ego calmly talked tactics while the other knew that all this energy was moonshine. One half of me was convinced that all this was real; the other knew it was illusion.

When I returned to camp to find the men in marching order on parade, an orderly thrust into my hand an in-telligence report saying that the Germans had doubled their frontline posts. Two German companies were now holding the front I was to attack with one. Towards dusk we marched out by platoons. Men going into action sup-port themselves by a sort of enforced hysterical cheerful-ness, but no one could be cheerful in the Third Battle of Ypres. I marched with Serjeant Walker (acting company serjeant-major) at the head of the company, and we talked quietly of other marches into battle. As always, when anticipation at last gave way to action, I found my mind clearing. The mental numbness of the last few days had given place to a numbness in the pit of the stomach. I was not now afraid, though I had a growing presentiment that I should be wounded. We crossed the Ypres canal, turned east at International Corner and presently led off the road in single file along a trench-board track. A battery of heavy howitzers fired over our heads as we left the road, the shock and flash almost blowing us flat in the mud. Before long the inevitable checks began in the column, and where we halted the ground was pitted with ominous new shell-holes, reeking of high explosives and powdered with brown grains of freshly scattered earth. In such a place one waited with impatience. Talbot, the adjutant, imperturbable as ever, strolled down the column and gossiped, but we could find little to look forward to with optimism. At Cheddar Villa we left the track and closed on the St. Julien Road. It was dark enough for the gun-teams to bring up supplies of ammunition, and the road was crowded with limbers and strings of pack-mules. As we approached St. Julien there was some confusion when platoons lost touch; mules and men and wagons crowded in the narrow way, until where the culvert passed over the Steenbeek the traffic jammed, shoulder to wheel. This was a windy moment, for on this line the Boche guns were laid and here from time to time they dropped hurricane barrages of shell-fire. Indeed, a few shells had already fallen to our right, and massacre might come at any minute; but we got through in safety. Beyond the Steen-beek there were no roads: guides led us by marked tracks among the shell-holes past the pill-box called Springfield and over the low ridge which had once been the Lange-marck-Gheluvelt line. Our jumping-off place lay down the forward slope marked by the tape laid two nights before. To find the way in the dark was a task worthy of Bunyan's pilgrim: "the pathway was here also exceeding narrow, and therefore good Christian was the more put to it; for when he sought in the dark, to shun the ditch on the one

106

hand, he was ready to tip over into the mire on the other.
Thus he went on, for the pathway was here so dark, that
oft-times, when he lifted up his foot to set forward, he
knew not where, nor upon what, he should set it next.
And ever and anon the flame and smoke would come out
in such abundance, with sparks and hideous noises . . .
thus he went on a great while; yet still the flames would be
reaching towards him: Also he heard doleful voices and
rushings to and fro, so that sometimes he thought he
should be torn to pieces, or trodden down like mire in
the streets."

§ 2

The four platoons found their way to their places, two
in front and two behind, a movement which they had so
often practised on a similar piece of ground thirty miles
away. I, after some deliberation, decided to pass the night
at Stroppe Farm, a forlorn heap of broken timber under
which was a sort of hutch or den in which it was safe to
show a light. My company had two other officers, Kerr
and Sinker, for Thorburn, who has already been mentioned, had been left behind in reserve. The two joined
their platoons, while I crawled under the wreckage to find
the hutch already occupied by Captain Morshead of the
16th Battalion, whose company adjoined mine on the left;
nor was I unwilling to share with him and not spend the
night alone. It was damp and not cold. With little help
from me Morshead chatted on, and I remember that I
paid him five francs which he had lent me. Once in the
night I went out to make a round of the company posi-

tions, but when the enemy started dropping shells into our area I was glad to take refuge in a little dry trench which No. 6 platoon had found. This platoon was more pleasant to visit than the others lying exposed to shell-fire in the open.

An hour before dawn the gas projectors on the hill behind went off with bright flashes, hurling opened cylinders of gas on to the enemy position at Winchester 1,000 yards away, and warning us that the time was short. Morshead wished me good luck and went to his battle position; I sent word to Sinker to take the morning rum issue round the platoons, and was then left to dissemble before my orderlies. At this stage I found myself fidgety and restless, longing for zero hour when, I believed, the worst would soon be over. I was preparing to make a final round of the platoons when an enemy shell whizzed evilly overhead and burst near the centre of my second wave.[1] No shell during the night had fallen so close. While I hesitated to distinguish what particular target was being fired on before choosing my path, there began a ghostly procession of "whizzbangs," whining sounds neither very fast nor very loud, as if they came from batteries well behind the German lines, but sounds which ended each in the sharp roar and metallic clang of shrapnel bursting on the slope behind me. I resigned myself to waiting for the end of a "morning strafe," and began to think that I might get my "blighty one"[2] without the added unpleasantness of going over the top. It was now about twenty minutes before zero, which was to be six o'clock.

[1] My company was to advance in two "waves", each of two platoons, the second wave being drawn up a hundred yards behind the first.

[2] Blighty—a soldier's corruption of the Hindustani word for one's native district. Hence used for England by soldiers serving abroad. A blighty wound is one serious enough to send you back to England.

As the shells came faster and faster, crashing into the waste of mud and hedge-stumps which hid our assembled brigade, I could not disguise from myself that the Boches had forestalled us with a full-dress bombardment of our jumping-off line. I began to wonder whether a Boche attack was coming, ignorant of ours; or whether (and this frightened me the more) they had learned our plans and would shatter our huddled groups—as they had done in August—before we left our lines. Should I visit the platoons in this shell-storm, or should I stay in my battle-position in touch with battalion headquarters? I decided to stay, believing that our own attack, thrown into confusion by the shelling, must break down, wondering whether there might be new orders, a postponement, a change of plan.

In the meanwhile I emerged from the hut beneath the fallen rafters and got down into a rude trench where two shell-holes had been joined together. With me one orderly, Lewis, crouched, looking more frightened than I thought I looked; the others with Serjeant Walker crouched behind the ruins ten yards away. When I shouted to them they replied cheerily and were more hopeful for the rest of the company than I was. I waited stolidly; Lewis shifted uneasily.

Suddenly the sky behind us threw up a stab of flame! A roll of thunder like the last trump itself opened with some few single blows and steadied into a throbbing roar. The shells screamed overhead so thick and fast they seemed to eclipse the sky as with an invisible roof, rumbling like earthquakes behind, crashing like a thousand cymbals before us, a pillar of fire against the dark sky, a pillar of cloud against the dawning east—leading us on!

It was zero hour and our barrage had fallen, blotting out the German bombardment with a drumfire forty times as great; there was no more thought or feeling, no more fear or doubt; only an endless blast of sound; a flicker of flame in the sky, a roaring and howling of shells over our heads, and a smoky pall of shrapnel.

My brain cleared though my ears were singing; the plan stood in my mind like a picture: I wondered how many men were left to carry it out. We must follow hard on the barrage and be on the enemy before they had recovered from the first shock of it. I jumped out of the trench, shouting to my little group, and together we stumbled forward towards the enemy. Behind me came Serjeant Walker, my servant Stanley, three runners, Lewis, Campbell and Greenwood, and then the signallers struggling with their gear and quickly falling behind. Looking round I can see no one else, no sign of human life or activity; but who cares? Skirting round shell-holes, and straggling over rough ground in half darkness, our group loses all order and trails after me in single file. There looms up in front a bank undercut by a row of dug-outs, familiar enough by the map. I draw my revolver, but they are smashed and empty. Over and on behind the thunder and lightning of the barrage. (Like cannon balls rolled down sheets of iron over our heads.) One is thankful for a steel helmet.

Through the tumult I isolate a distinct noise, a spitting, a crackling, like children's fireworks. Rifle bullets! Phut! Phut! Small arms indeed! We look about vaguely. It seems to have grown already a little lighter, so that lumps loom up irregularly in front thirty yards away—half left. Heads! Three or four heads of Boches in a shell-hole shooting at us! We see them together. Stanley shouts and brandishes his bayonet. Then I see Campbell lying curled up and grey-faced at my feet. Why, he's dead! And by God, they've hit "Tiny" Greenwood. He is staggering about and bellowing, his hand on his chest. Stanley catches and lowers him to the ground behind the stunted ruins of a

110

hedge-row which gives a little cover. Crack, crack, crack, come the bullets at thirty yards' range, aimed more distinctly every moment as the light grows and the barrage lifts ahead. The enemy are even near enough to throw a bomb. Stanley and I fumble with field-dressings. There are now only three of us and three or four Boches shooting at us from cover. At least let's quiet this poor lad's confounded roaring and then make a plan. Poor "Tiny" Greenwood, the smallest man in the company and the willingest. I remember my morphine tablets and give him one, two and three till he is silent. Stanley rises and shouts again, "Come on, sir, let's go for the swine." "No," I say, "get down in this shell-hole," and I am right. There is no chance for three men to charge three over the mud and pitfalls. Stanley plucks me by the sleeve and says plaintively. "Aw, come on, sir." Walker and I get down in the hole and begin to shoot though Stanley stands and calls us once more. "Come down, you fool," I order him. Then he comes down, slithering on the edge of the shell-hole, dropping his rifle with a clatter. A bullet has hit him in the eye, smashing his left brow and cheek-bone into a ghastly hole. I am dumbfounded with rage and horror. They have got Stanley, best of friends and loyallest of servants, and my last orderly. Walker and I are pent up in this hole and dare not move. Stanley is dead, who has always supported me, Stanley who gave me confidence in myself.

I sat stupidly in the half-light, not looking at my servant's body, and then vaguely imitated Walker, who was firing on the Boches when they showed their heads. I must have emptied my revolver before this time, and now picked up Stanley's rifle, coated with mud from fixed bayonet to stock. With difficulty I fired a round or two, wrenching at the clogged mechanism after each shot. Walker gave a cry of joy as he got one Boche through

111

the head, but one or two more ran up from neighbouring shell-holes and made the odds still heavier against us. Still our own guns thundered overhead, and now the German guns began to reassert themselves, dropping a few shells experimentally in their own lines, which they guessed had fallen into our hands. The stubborn group confronting us still held their place under fire of their own artillery. Ceasing to fire at us except when we showed our heads, they sent up signal rockets to give their position to their own observers.

But for the roaring of our own shrapnel two hundred yards away, there was no sign of English activity. No other Englishman could be seen or heard, and, fatal event, we had "lost the barrage." In the midst of a great battle ours was an independent duel. Down in a shell-hole where the view was restricted by towering ridges and ramps of thrown-up earth, we had the limited vision of the mole. There must have been ten thousand men hidden in the landscape, though we had not seen ten. I began to wonder whether our attack had been dstroyed and was to be the tragedy of to-morrow's *communiqué* in the German Press. "Yesterday after intense drumfire the English attacked east of Ypres and were driven back to their lines by our gallant 'field greys'." Perhaps, even, my own group was the only one which had advanced, in which case we might be able to hide here all day and creep back at dusk, to the remnants of the shattered battalion. How could the day be not lost now that the shrapnel banged so far ahead and no one seemed to be advancing? As we waited in the broadening light time passed—seconds or hours, we had no conception, till we heard voices behind us, a Lewis-gun rattling, and a reserve platoon at hand. I shouted to them to support us by outflanking this group of Germans, and as we opened fire again, invisible Lewis-gunners crept closer over the mountainous shell-holes. The Boches ceased fire. At that moment Walker leaped up with a shout and began to shoot in a new direction. Following his aim I saw straight to the front and a hundred yards away a crowd of men running towards us in grey uniforms. Picking up another rifle I joined him in pouring rapid fire into this counter-attack. We saw one at least drop, to Walker's rifle I think, then noticed that they were running with their hands held up. Laughing, we emptied our magazines at them in spite of that, but at this point one of my favourite N.C.O.s, Corporal Fell, came tumbling into the shell-hole, hit through both thighs and bearing the pain with no more than a grunt or two. While I was trying to bandage his four wounds with one field dressing, and he to explain how his Lewis-gun had appeared to save us, I forgot the crowd of "Kamerads." Just as I was telling him to crawl home as best he could, twenty or thirty Germans came running up with that shambling gait and bucolic manner I had always noticed in them, emphasised by the awkward gesture of their raised hands. The nearest had not seen me in the shell-hole, and as he approached, noticing a red cross on his arm I reached up and pulled him up short by the skirt of his greatcoat with a jerk that frightened him out of his wits. "Ambulance," I said, pointing to the wounded corporal. Then hardly stopping to see more, Walker and I rose, collected the Lewis-gun and its team and continued our advance. The surrendering Germans carried back our wounded men and we barely noticed in the excitement that the four snipers who had held us up so long slipped into the crowd of captives and went away with them. We should certainly not have given them quarter if we had thought of it in time.

Once out of our burrow the scene was changed. The long rolling valley was visible again running down to the brook called the Stroombeek, and on the rising slope towards Winchester the shrapnel of our barrage was now

113

bursting, making a picture more like a battle in the "Illustrated London News." In full daylight at last we could see scattered parties of men advancing and none of them very far in front of us. Again my hesitations vanished and I led the way towards our objective. Before we had gone a hundred yards we met two serjeants of A company, both old friends, a little lost with their platoons, but not at all disconcerted. I ordered them to stay there and dig in, for the battalion seemed very scattered and it seemed wise to consolidate these gains, in a battle where the Boche was very quick to counter-attack. While they obeyed and chose a position unwillingly, I halted to write a report and mark up a situation map; then leaving my Lewis-gun with the serjeants I continued to advance with Serjeant Walker and two or three men. On our right were Colonial troops attacking in much greater strength than ours, so that my own front looked empty but theirs crowded with men, and before long one of their platoons came straying across my front. It suddenly struck me that the platoon commander was a friend whom I had not seen since I was a child; I seized him by the hand and introduced myself. As we exchanged civilities I became aware that we were under machine-gun fire. I was explaining that he had gone astray when this diversion occurred in his proper direction, and hastily clapping him on the back, I sent him off with his men to strafe the machine-gun, an order which he willingly obeyed. This odd incident, evidence of the unreal state of mind engendered by the excitement of battle, passed from my memory, to drift up again into my consciousness a few days later, blurred like the remembrance of a dream so that I have never been able to recall my old friend's face and do not know who he was. At least the machine-gun shortly ceased to fire.

Several other groups of men were now converging with us on a rough path of planks across the marshy Stroombeek. Here we fell in with Flint of C company, still commanding a whole platoon, and hence we sent back another message to headquarters by a machine-gun officer who had reconnoitred his position and was returning for his guns. Crossing the bridge we deployed half left and advanced up a slope towards some wreckage which we took to be Albatross or Wellington Farm. Under heavy shell-fire and some distant machine-gun fire we skirmished up the slope from hole to hole, till Flint reached the ruin and dugout that we thought was Wellington; but to our surprise it was already in English hands. It had been taken by a platoon of A company who were delighted at having captured a German anti-tank gun. For the last few minutes the battle had really been proceeding according to plan. Still like a man in a dream I had been commanding and even manœuvring considerable bodies of men, mostly, it must be admitted, of neighbouring companies. The advance was orderly and regular, and recorded in formal written messages which I sent back at intervals to headquarters; and we were near our objective. Having checked with the other officers our position on the map and decided that my proper place was two hundred yards to the left, I moved away with the last survivors of my company to get in touch again with Captain Morshead of the 16th, who had spent the night with me at Stroppe Farm. On the crest of the rise we caught up our own barrage and halted where the banging, smashing shrapnels were bursting on the first objective. Presently we edged farther to the left, because one of our guns was consistently firing short and dropping shells among us. Topping the rise I saw before me two smashed pill-boxes among gigantic shell-holes. I picked up here a German automatic pistol. In the shadow of the pill-box was lying the body of a British officer, which proved that we were again in touch with our own people. Beyond it we found a party of the 16th Battalion consolidating an

115

enormous shell-hole. We had met exactly on the flank of our objective.

§ 3

We selected a large shell-hole under the lee of the broken pill-box of Winchester for my few men and those of the 16th, and settled down to resist the probable counter-attack. Soon Hesketh, an officer of the 16th, arrived with a Reserve platoon and my handful became an insignificant detail of the defence. My last Lewis gun I had left to cover our advance; several men had been sent with messages; until at one time, of all the company, Serjeant Walker, the company sanitary man, Bridgwater, who had drifted in from somewhere or other, and I, were the only representatives; and though we had got here first we soon began to feel that we were merely getting in the way of the 16th. Hesketh was very much junior to me, but he had his men well in hand, and organised them briskly, as sentries or at deepening the shell-hole. There was very little for me to do except to send even Serjeant Walker away to look for any more of my company. We were disappointed to find that a large party of men moving up in artillery formation was not our second wave but D company, all of whose officers were hit and who were now lost. Then a trench mortar battery came forward to take up a position near us; but no third wave passed through to follow the barrage which now fell three hundred yards ahead.

The morning wore on. Attackers and defenders at this point had spent their force. We had got our objective and were too ludicrously weak to move again. A few shells were coming over and a persistent sniper fired occasionally, his bullets crashing into the ruins of the pill-box beside us. Away to the left we saw two British tanks crawling forward into Poelcapelle, the only signs of battle except the fire curtain in front and the thunders rolling perpetually overhead.[1]

A major of the 16th, came striding over the shell-holes alone, reconnoitring the front. He pointed out the open country before us and tried to make me advance. As I had no men, a strong position and my final objective, I refused to move, at which he looked disgusted. He walked round the pill-box, the Boche sniper viciously firing at him, glanced at the body we had seen lying there, and called to me that it was Captain Morshead, still alive. I went out and found the latter shot through the neck, no doubt by that same sniper, and hardly conscious. I gave him some water, and called two men who brought him into the shell-hole, where, after being bandaged by the stretcher-bearers, he recognised us and tried to speak. Soon they carried him down the line; and he died in hospital, the day after being awarded the Military Cross.

Towards midday, the enemy shelling really began. Black shrapnels crashed overhead and huge crumps burst round us among the ruins. We all crouched down in our one huge shell-hole, which I began to regret, as a single shell in it would kill us all. One or two men were hit; especially, I remember, one who was standing up with his sleeves rolled up, when a shrapnel burst right above us. A sliver of steel came down and hit him lengthwise on the bare forearm, making a clean cut three inches long between the two bones, as if his arm had been slit with a knife. To my horror the wound gaped open like a freshly cut shoulder of mutton. Though this was as "cushy" a wound as man could desire, the sight of it cured me of hoping for a "blighty one." The victim agreed with me, for he danced and cried out with the pain.

[1] The Contact aeroplane flew over about this time to discover how far we had advanced; we lighted flares for it.

117

My Lewis-gunners were now in position close by, and it seemed that the best way to reduce the crowd in the shell-hole was to go away myself. Hesketh didn't want me and showed it; goodness knows, I didn't want to stay there; so, by agreement with the major who passed that way again, I decided to leave my Lewis Gun section with Hesketh while Serjeant Walker and I withdrew to Stroppe Farm to pick up stragglers, and reorganise. So Walker, Bridgwater and I turned back down the hill through very heavy shell-fire, across the Stroombeek, and over the plain, now scattered with grey drifting clouds of smoke from high-explosive shells. Hardly out of the swamp we ran into Lance-Corporal Reese of No. 7 platoon with a few men and another gun. They were all that was left of the platoon, and had dug in, satisfied that they had reached their objective. At last we got back to Stanley's body, where I stopped not without a shudder to remove my glasses, all spattered with brains and blood, from his shoulder; I had to leave the strap, which was too gruesome to carry. Then we found our company stretcher-bearers performing prodigies of work, in spite, they were convinced, of being under deliberate German shell-fire, and using the little trench where I had visited one of my platoons last night as a rendezvous. I forthwith relieved the leading spirit of this party of noncombatant duty to make him an acting section-commander.[1] In this trench I made my headquarters, and we tried to learn the situation. One officer, Sinker, seemed to have been hit while taking round the rum at the jumping-off place; a serjeant and a corporal went down wounded before zero. Otherwise the company started well. They all found groups of Germans resisting long and bravely in the front line. Another serjeant was killed early, and a third badly hit

[1] He received the Military Medal after this action.

in the face. My own party had a typical experience. Kerr with No. 8 platoon got farther forward, killed some Boches, and was shot himself in a hand-to-hand encounter.

A man called Whitworth came from the Lewis-gun section still at Winchester to ask if they were to stay there. He was a good fellow, and after discussing the situation with him I told him to wait till I had reported the company's condition to battalion headquarters.

Always very nervous when alone under shell-fire, and badly shaken after the day's experiences and the bombardment at Winchester, I found the walk of two or three hundred yards to Victoria Farm terrifying. Shells seemed to pursue me up the slope, and catch me when no deep shell-hole was near. I floundered in oceans of knee-deep mud and flung myself flat, when one shell fell close, on what looked like fairly solid ground, but turned out to be as thin as half-cooked porridge. So the whole front of me from the chest down was soaked through and coated with slime.

At last I struggled up to the little half-broken pill-box called Victoria and went in. The Colonel and Adjutant were plainly very pleased to see me. From their account I was able at last to get some sort of general picture of the battle. All our objectives had been reached and a hundred and fifty Germans taken prisoner, but at a cost in casualties which had shattered the battalion. All the severest fighting had been in the first few minutes, which had seen a score of petty duels like my own, group against group among the shell-holes. Most of our officers and N.C.O.s were hit, and until I came they had counted me too a casualty, all the messages which I had proudly composed in such careful military form having gone astray. They gave me the good news that Thorburn, my reserve officer, had been sent for and would join me to-night, and the bad news, too, that, casualties or no casualties, we were not to be relieved for three days. The Colonel suggested that when Thorburn arrived I should come and join them in the dugout to get some sleep. Then he came out with me and we returned to the remnants of my company.

More tragedies! While I was away Whitworth had been sitting above the trench talking. In the dusk he was suddenly silent. No one had noticed a shell splinter from some far-away burst fly over and hit him in the head. He was breathing when we arrived, but, the stretcher-bearers said, as good as dead already. Nevertheless, they took him down to the dressing-station. The poor devils were beat after saving lives all day.

Then I settled down in the little trench, about twelve feet long and six feet deep and wonderfully dry, to wait for Thorburn who arrived with a runner about eight o'clock very cheery. We agreed that our conversation a week before had proved prophetic: the battalion had taken a nasty knock this time. Leaving him in charge I returned to Victoria, where the C.O. shared a tin of hot food with me, my first square meal that day. Armstrong, the intelligence officer, took me in hand with an endless story about himself, the C.O. and a wounded Boche.

"When I was going round with the C.O. this morning after you'd gone over we found a wounded Boche lying in the mud—down there by the Stroombeek where you couldn't get him out. He was dying, I should think."

"Yes," said I sleepily, "there were hundreds."

"Well, this one," Armstrong continued, "he was done for, squirming, the poor devil was, and anyhow there was no chance of getting him down to a dressing-station from there. Best to put him out of his misery, you'd say, wouldn't you, Edmonds?"

120

"Yes, I suppose so; let's get some sleep."

"Oh, well," said Armstrong, "just wait. Damn funny it was. We found this Boche: there was the C.O. and me and a runner; and the C.O. said to the runner, 'You'd best shoot the poor fellow,' and the Boche just lay there and groaned. He knew. But, you know, the runner couldn't do it. He unslung his rifle and fingered the trigger and just couldn't do it. So the C.O. turned to me and when it came to the point no more could I: so the C.O. drew his gun himself and went up to the Boche and looked fierce, and the Boche squirmed and I'm damned if the C.O. didn't weaken too. Damn funny, wasn't it? And we just left him there, so I suppose he'll die in the mud to-night."

But by this time I was asleep, having found a quiet corner. It was luxury for five of us to lie down on a concrete floor in a cellar only fifteen feet square and with no door, that chilly autumn evening.

In the morning I went out early to my men, and found all well and Thorburn a tower of strength. While we were cooking breakfast on a "Tommy's cooker."[1] General Hutchinson with a staff officer and his galloper came wandering up from the rear, and in full view of the enemy. He talked cheerily to us, as always, and then pointed out a wounded Boche in a little hollow, a few yards away, whose legs were shattered and who was trying to walk on his knees with two crutches of broken timber. We had known of this man before, but were leaving him until our own wounded were all in. "Hutchy" insisted on our attending to this man first. Then he wandered on fearlessly to the front.

Orders came soon to move up to the Stroombeek and dig in a second line. We were now to be support company. Thorburn and I went on first, and Serjeant Walker followed with the company. The ground was very bad and

[1] A portable spirit stove small enough to go in the pocket.

strewn with bodies, many more German than English as we grimly noted. Round Kerr's objective, where we settled in a group of shell-holes, they lay especially thick. Someone volunteered to find No. 8 platoon's Lewis-gun section, which was supposed to have dug in near by. It arrived presently—several men with a self-appointed leader, a lanky dark youth, new to the company and never in action before, who had been with Kerr and described the latter's gallantry and end. Seeing that the N.C.O.s were all killed, he had taken charge of the gun and the section (since there was no very senior man among them); he had finished off this party of Germans; had gone forward to his correct objective, dug in and remained there through the night, and most wonderful of all, had kept his gun in action and cleaned it, in that mud. I am prepared to swear it was the only clean gun in the Ypres salient. He had found his objective, merely from his platoon-commander's description of it, while most of us officers, having pored over maps for weeks past, and reconnoitred the ground in advance, could find our way to nowhere at all. He knew exactly where everything was and appreciated the tactical position perfectly.[1] So I put this prodigy, confirmed in the command of his section, to watch the crossing of the Stroombeek.

Thorburn and I drifted over to a hedge beside the stream, and got in touch with D company on our right, in some remains of trenches near Albatross, which turned out to be not a pill-box but a ruined dugout of logs and earth. Having lost their way they had never come into action yesterday.

From there we followed the swampy stream along to a little newly discovered pill-box. This had lain unsuspected in our area, but had been captured by the Colonials, who were much thicker on the ground than we were and had

[1] He received the Military Medal after this action.

122

squeezed us over towards the left. Marriott and Flint were just taking this sector over from them with the remains of C company, about twenty of our men relieving fifty or sixty of theirs under a cheerful middle-aged officer, who was very thankful for the help our stretcher-bearers had given him. His men had dug quite a good continuous trench in the night, in dead ground just behind the low crest of the eastern bank of the Stroombeek.

Wolfe, who had come up from reserve to take charge of D company, Thorburn, and I then settled in a shell-hole near my company, which had now risen to about twenty-five strong. The fourth Lewis-gun had been found with the sole survivor of the team, who, of course, had no ammunition, but had dug in for the night and was apparently prepared to stay in position whether the gun would fire or not. But no more N.C.O.s came in. Both officers, all four platoon serjeants, eleven out of twelve section commanders had been hit; only Serjeant Walker and I and Lance-Corporal Reese, whose stripe was not a week old, were left. No wonder the company was a little scattered.

Though the day had started well, it was to turn out the most wretched of my life. The three of us crouched happily enough in our circular pit, five feet in diameter, and dug it down till it was five feet deep. We talked of what people do talk of in such situations, "shop," the chance of relief, yesterday's adventures, to-day's expectations, details of administration, and sometimes reminiscences. We knew there would be heavy shelling sooner or later, but felt disinclined to discuss that. One had a curious undefined superstition that to mention it might attract it.

As we were in full view of the enemy on the right front, along the valley of the Stroombeek, the movement of men

123

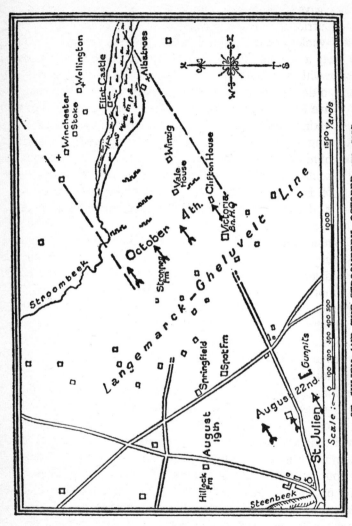

ST. JULIEN AND THE STROOMBEEK, OCTOBER 4TH, 1917.
A landscape of mud and water-logged shell-holes. The small squares represent German pill boxes.

124

in and near our position drew its reward. When the German gunners really settled down to their day's shooting they gave us their fullest attention. There was no drumfire, no hurricane barrage, but a steady slow bombardment of the whole valley with heavies; all day the fire grew in intensity and accuracy; and occasionally the area was raked over with a finer shower of field-gun shells. We had nothing to do but sit and listen for the roar of the 5.9's, lasting for five seconds each, perhaps twice a minute. One would be talking aimlessly of some unimportant thing when the warning would begin. The speaker's voice would check for an infinitesimal fraction of a second; then he would finish his sentence with a studied normality marvellously true to life. Everyone listened hard to the conversation, but with more than half an ear cocked in the direction of the enemy. If the shell were coming close, one would crouch down against the side of the pit, apparently as a mere perfunctory precaution, actually with delight that one could take cover unashamed. When the shell had burst in a smother of black smoke, and the clods and whining splinters had ceased to fall pattering around, one went on with the conversation. It was a kind of round game, in which a man felt he had lost a point every time a grunt or a remark about the danger was fetched out of him.

Thorburn won easily; of course he had been through nothing yet but a night in a safe, dry trench. Yet this trial might well have finished off a fresh man. The shells fell consistently among our men (who, however, were well scattered and in the deepest shell-holes); every other one would fling a shower of mud on to our helmets. About one in five or six would fall near enough to shake the parapet, blast its pungent fumes in our faces, and set every nerve in our bodies jangling. Wolfe came out in an unexpected light; he was a tall, pale, flabby medical student in spectacles, and until that day I had had but a poor opinion of him. Every time a shell fell near he proceeded to tell us that he had a very strong presentiment; nothing was going to hit him that day. He said it so often, with such conviction, and so ingenuously, that it cheered me wonderfully. even at the worst moments. He did nothing and seemed to care little, but was quite contented about himself.

I needed some cheering up. I had had very much worse times than either of the others, but cannot deceive myself, all the same; I never could stand shell-fire. I got into a thoroughly neurotic state during the day. Enduring a bombardment is the opportunity for that kind of nervous disease which made Dr. Johnson touch every post as he walked along Fleet Street. You think of absurd omens and fetishes to ward off the shell you hear coming. A strong inward feeling compels you to sit in a certain position, to touch a particular object, to whistle so many bars of a tune silently between your teeth. If you complete the charm in time you are safe—until the next one. This absurdity becomes a dark, overpowering fatalism. You contemplate with horror that you have made a slip in the self-imposed ritual, or that the augury sign of your own invention shows against you. You imagine that the shells are more deliberate and accurate than could be possible. They seem to have a volition of their own and to wander malevolently until they see a target on which to pounce; they seem to hurl themselves with intention sounding in the fierce roar of their near approach; they defy your mute relief when they fall far away, by sending slivers of jagged steel sighing and murmuring hundreds of yards towards you, long after the shock of the explosion is spent and gone.

Every gun and every kind of projectile had its own personality. Old soldiers always claimed that they knew the calibre of a shell by its sound and could always foretell

126

which shells were going to fall dangerously close. Yet far more than they calculated depended on the range and the nature of the intervening ground. Sometimes a field-gun shell would leap jubilantly with the pop of a champagne cork from its muzzle, fly over with a steady buzzing crescendo, and burst with a fully expected bang; sometimes a shell would be released from a distant battery of heavies to roll across a huge arc of sky, gathering speed and noise like an approaching express train, ponderous and certain. Shells flying over valleys and woods echoed strangely and defied anticipation; shells falling in enclosed spaces simply arrived with a double bang and no warning at all. Some shells whistled, others shrieked, others wobbled through space gurgling like water poured from a decanter.

So all the day you listened, calculated, hoped or despaired, making imaginary bargains with fate, laying odds with yourself on the chances of these various horrors. One particular gun would seem to be firing more directly on you than the others. You would wait for its turn so intently as to forget other perhaps more real dangers. At last it comes. You hold frenziedly on to the conversation; you talk a little too fast; your nerves grow tense, and while you continue to look and talk like a man, your involuntary muscles get a little out of hand. Are your knees quivering a little? Are you blinking? Is your face contorted with fear? You wonder and cannot know. Force yourself to do something, say something, think something, or you will lose control. Get yourself in hand with some voluntary action. Drum out a tune with your finger-tips upon your knee. Don't hurry—keep time—get it finished, and you will be safe this once. Here superstition and neurasthenia step in. Like the child who will not walk on the lines in the pavement and finds real safety in putting each foot on a square stone you feel that your ritual protects you. As the roar of an approaching shell rises nearer and louder you listen in inward frenzy to the shell, in outward calm to the conversation. Steady with those nervous drum-taps on your knee; don't break time or the charm is broken and the augury vain. The shell roars near. What is Thorburn saying?

"Oh yes! The rations came up at nine o'clock, enough for twice our numbers." (Explosion!)

Thank God, the tune was finished soon enough. But then comes an overwhelming rush of panic. The next shell will be the nearest, the climax of the day. What is the next shell when the air is never free from their sound? The next that is at all near. But how near? Which is near enough to break the tension? Thorburn is saying, "We haven't issued the rum to-day. Best do it at dusk, don't you think?" (Terrific explosion!) "God," you say with a gasp, dropping for an instant the mask of indifference. You eye the others guiltily and wonder if they are going through the same performance. At least are you keeping up appearances as well as they do? What a comfort that Wolfe's augury is so optimistic.

Once in the afternoon I was on the point of breaking down. My luck turned; the self-deluding charm failed; omens were bad and a shell roared into the mud throwing clods and whining splinters on our heads. I swore and moved nervously and lost control of my features.

"Steady," said Thorburn, putting a hand on my arm.

That was my nadir. The shelling slackened and stopped, until between Wolfe's optimism and Thorburn's unconcern I revived my good spirits.

It rained that evening. The sides of the shell-hole first became slimy, then crumbled away in schloops of mud, then began to be hollowed out in channels by little rivulets of water. Our dry foothold became a puddle. The water dripped off the rim of our helmets into the back of our necks. In spite of all precautions the skirts of our rain-coats slopped mud on to our knees. The last stronghold of dryness was defeated in the end when a puddle formed on the ledge behind me and I soaked the seat of my trousers. There was no prospect of getting dry or of sitting in a dry place for eighty-and-forty hours. The ground, which had been thick and soggy like porridge, now became thin and sloppy like soup. In moving about one had been able to walk on the dry rims of the shell-holes and to avoid the sludgy bottoms of them. Now one walked on sludgy ridges to avoid the pools of water in every hole. The Stroombeek, a miserable little drainage ditch, which the bombardment had scattered into a bog thirty yards wide, spread wider and wetter still.

Soon after dark, Newsom of A company came slopping through the mud with five or six men. He was lost (everybody was always lost in the dark) and looking for his company in a little trench near Albatross. He was even shorter of men than we were, and persuaded me to lend him Lance-Corporal Reese, which I did, to help a front-line company. Then feeling that I ought to do something, I rashly offered to guide him to the pill-box at C company headquarters, from where he could easily find his own way. A hedge-row ran from my position to the Stroombeek, and along this we started. We had only a hundred yards to go. The swamp was wetter and the stream broader than in the morning. We wandered on, wading ankle deep,

129

treading on roots or mounds of mud when we could find them. It seemed a long way. We got too deep into the water and struck to the right again to find the bank; but there was no dry place, just an endless swamp—puddles, mud, chaos. The earth was without form and void. I had to admit that I was lost.

We wandered vaguely; it was as dark as the Pit.

Presently a British battery opened fire, dropping shells unpleasantly close in front of us. We must be right up to the front line then, such front line as there was. A smart bombardment began, which forced us to crouch down, for we could take no proper cover in this marsh. (There are no words in English for the omnipresent wetness, the sliminess, the stickiness of the mud, the gouts that you found clogging your fingers, and wiped off accidentally in your hair when you adjusted your helmet, the smears of it that appeared on your clean message forms and your mess-tin, the saturation of your clothes with its semi-solid filthiness, the smell of it, and the taste of it, and the colour of it.)

As we could only expect, the German guns began to retaliate. We were not reassured to find ourselves between the two fires. The Boche shells fell close behind us, the English close in front; we had wandered out into No Man's Land.

We moved about trying to avoid the danger, and soon became entirely confused as to direction. The shells whizzed down from all sides, bursting with red showers of sparks and whiffs of smoke, and, difficult as it was to locate it in the dark, we endeavoured to find the empty vortex of the storm. We were helpless here for some un-measured time, wet through, cold and paddling through seas of slime, in absolute blackness broken only by the occasional gleam of a high bursting shell.

At last in a slight lull I caught sight of rising ground,

and led the party in that direction, where we came into an area of big shell-holes, that is, a planless maze of high ridges and pits where it was impossible to see more than five yards in any direction. I was leading, not more than three paces ahead of the next man, when another whirl of shell-fire came down.

They flung themselves one way into cover, I another.

In a few seconds, when I stood up again, they had vanished.

"Newsom!" I called, not too loud, for this was No Man's Land. No answer.

I circled round, looking for them. They cannot have been more than thirty yards away, but in that noise, darkness and chaos, they were undiscoverable. At last I gave them up, found a good piece of cover where I could watch in their supposed direction, and waited for something to happen.

In time, the shelling stopped. I wondered where I was, and how to get back through the lines. For all I knew, there might be a German sentry-group three feet away in the next shell-hole. I wasn't even sure which was east and which was west, though I was inclined to think we had missed our way by edging off too far to the right, southward from the Stroombeek.

My troubles were soon solved for me, when the clouds broke above and I caught a pale glimpse of the Pole Star. Now to apply the invariable rule—east for Germany and west for "Blighty." Not for the first time I kept the Pole Star on my right hand and walked straight for home.

So long a time passed before I came to anything, and so quiet was the night now, that I came to the conclusion I was through the lines and would find nothing till I got to the Canal Bank,[1] but at last I came to a white tape

[1] The Ypres salient was an arc of which the chord was the Ypres-Comines Canal.

laid out on the ground, leading in my direction. I followed it for ages and ages, seeing and hearing no one. When I thought I must be out of the battlefield the tape ended abruptly not far from a pill-box, to which I went to enquire my way. The man at the door told me it was "headquarters."

"What headquarters? Brigade?"

"No, sir, our battalion, of course."

I had walked right up to the door without knowing it; and here came Talbot the Adjutant out to see who I was. Good old Pole Star!

Talbot was just going up on a tour of inspection and we agreed to go round the lines together till we reached my position. A party of stragglers, including Bridgwater, whom I had found wandering alone in the attack yesterday and was lost again to-night, had been assembled at Headquarters to carry rations up to my company.

Talbot, who had a long trip in front of him, sent off the slow-going ration party with an orderly, to avoid the most dangerous spots and pick their way through the area under fire, while we two headed for the crossing of the Stroombeek. As we went up towards Winchester we found a section of A company, well forward, dug in and quite happy under a surly, independent corporal. They had been in touch with C company, but had seen nothing of their own for forty-eight hours, during which they had lived on shell-hole water and food from dead men's haversacks. They seemed prepared to stay there as long again. We went on and arrived at last at A company headquarters, to find Newsom also returned safe. Talbot went back, and I stayed to discuss the night's adventures, letting Thorburn know that I would return later.

There dawn found us, in a little bit of narrow trench partly covered with a sheet of iron; and there we sat for half an hour or so while a patrol of Boche planes flew backwards and forwards above us firing machine-guns and, attracting what was worse, a rain of splinters on our heads from the British anti-aircraft guns.

I determined quite basely to take shelter for a few hours in C company's pill-box, and presently plucked up courage and squattered across through the stream to it.

This pill-box was the only piece of good cover in the battalion area. Imagine a small room ten feet square and six feet high with walls of thick rough concrete. There is only one opening, the door, over which a waterproof sheet is draped. The furniture consists of four bunks made of wire stretched on wooden frames. Signallers and officers' servants have made a little hutch under the lee of the outer wall. Inside, live Marriott and Flint, a serjeant, and as many other people as are thought to deserve refuge. During the day Newsom and Wolfe each pay a visit to get some rest. I come first and stay longest. After all, the headquarters of a front-line company make quite a good command-post for a support company commander, and Thorburn's position is within shouting distance and full view by daylight. On such a little journey had we lost our way last night.

Flint is something in the same exhausted state as myself; Marriott, who came up from reserve with Thorburn and Wolfe after the attack, is very cheerful and doing most of the work. Their company is lined up fairly safe in the trench made by the Colonials. Neither trench nor pill-box is under direct observation from the front, though both are visible to the enemy farther over to the right. The open door of the pill-box faces that way.

Mariott welcomed me cordially enough, and found me the dry corner of a bed, where I tried to get an hour's sleep, but with little success. After a time he came into the pill-box, grinning, to ask me to take away some men of mine who were creating a disturbance in his trench. I

133

went out and found the ten ration-carriers of last night all roaring drunk. The poor devils had got lost, just like everyone else, had wandered all night, and finally decided that the company was annihilated. Not without good sense they decided not to starve. They did their best with a whole company's rations, but a whole company's rum defeated them. Hither they had wandered very happy and very sleepy, but rather inclined to sing themselves to sleep. We saved the rest of the food and rum, and sent over the remains, plenty for my handful of men.

It was difficult to know what to do with these men. One or two were helpless and comatose, one or two were incurably cheerful, the others varied from one extreme to the other. To arrest them and send them down the line would bring shell-fire on them and their escort, besides weakening the outposts. I stormed at them in my severest manner, promising them all courts-martial and death sentences. Some understood me and sobered a little, but Bridgwater and two or three others only blinked and looked more amiable than ever. If I had had any laughter in me I should have burst out laughing, too. We brought most of them round to a condition soon where they could go back to the company. The hopeless cases we left to sleep it off. There were no shooting parties at dawn, after all, as a sequel to this episode.

During the rest of the day I remained almost entirely in the pill-box. The shell-fire gradually increased as it had done yesterday, but we had no direct hits, any one of which would have done for us. Marriott kept up a running fire of conversation all day, little jokes and reminiscences, sly hints about my company and the rum, comparisons of our men with the Colonials, anecdotes of the day and of old battles. He had a N.C.O. in the pill-box with him, as orderly serjeant, one of those professional humorists without whom no company could hang together. The queer turns of his dialect, and an attractive little stuttering in his speech, an acute street-arab sense of humour, combined with the manners and deference of a gentleman, made him perhaps a perfect example of the urban soldier. The stories flowed out of him all day, his adventures with long-forgotten brigadiers, "madamaselles" or serjeant-majors, his friends and their idiosyncrasies, love and war and the weather, the bitterness of things, red tape and bad language. (I cannot refrain from quoting "that our armies swore terribly in Flanders.") He could tell a tale against a staff officer always with tact enough not to scandalise the officers present. If I were Dickens and could write down what he said, my fortune as a novelist would be made. But I'm afraid the jokes that made us reel with laughter would be flat to-day. One jumped at any excuse to be gay, and to laugh meant to forget that open door, facing the wrong way, through which a shell might come at any moment to burst in the midst of us. One message arrived from headquarters that made the mirth a little more spontaneous. An orderly of my company brought us word that the Berkshires were lending us a company which was to take over the front that night. The rest of us would be reorganised a few hundred yards back. We waited impatiently for dusk. One of our occupations was discussing what was the exact position of this pill-box. At first Flint had taken it for Wellington, one of his objectives, but we decided it must be one of two unnamed but suspected ones in the bed of the Stroombeek. After much poring over maps we decided that Wellington must be in front of us in No Man's Land, if not still in German hands. We thought it a good joke that in the night a sapper had ignorantly gone forward all alone, far beyond our advanced posts, and had nailed a notice-board, marked Wellington, on a tree-stump, not suspecting that he was in the enemies' lines. We had thought Wellington was

135

here; he had thought we were there. Then we talked of names for this one, and christened it Flint Castle at last with all due form.

At dusk when we were all ready the orderly arrived again. Where were the Berks? we asked. Not yet come up. But he had brought instead a large rough mongrel sheep dog, trained to carry messages through fire. Marriott grew quite despondent. "I thought they were going to send up the Berkshires," he said, "but all we're going to get now is barks"; at which we laughed uproariously. The Berks never did come, but before long a company of another regiment began to arrive. I collected my gear (we were in full marching order), and splashed through the stream to Thorburn, who had had another day's shelling and felt a little neglected. We headed back a second time to the jumping-off line, where we were now to be reserve company. Marriott withdrew his men to our position in the shell-holes by the Stroombeek.

As Thorburn and I ploughed through the mud after our men, we passed one of the relieving platoons going forward. Their subaltern gripped me by the arm.

"Who are you? Where are you going? Where's the front line? Have you seen A company?" he asked all in a rush.

"Keep straight on," I answered jauntily, "follow the tape. Your captain's up there. We've just been relieved."

"Don't go!" he said. "Don't leave us! For God's sake, show us the way."

I had met someone more frightened than myself. My confidence came back to me in a moment. This man was a shivering funk.

"God damn it!" I said. "You're all right. You're much stronger than we were. There's a good dugout up there— you can't miss it."

And I shook him off and walked on. I wonder what

state that poor devil was in at the end of his tour. But I had only gained a momentary confidence, and before morning was sinking back into the same apathy of suppressed fear as before. We took up our position on the right half of the jumping-off line, quite near headquarters. There were about twenty-seven men to organise in four sections, and place in the best shell-holes. For company headquarters Serjeant Walker, Thorburn and I found an old incomplete pill-box called on the map Cluster House. It was one of those early German efforts made of concrete on the western and of wood on the eastern side, so that in case of capture it would give no cover against German shell-fire. But it gave shelter from the rain, and here we settled. To make some amends to Thorburn for the twenty-four hours duty he had taken alone, I sent him to battalion headquarters to sleep, where they found him a corner of some kind. Walker took the top bunk in the little room, I took the lower one, but could only doze for an hour or two, in spite of the fact that I had not had eight hours' sleep out of the last ninety. It was very cold and I was acutely aware of my wet knees. At the first sign of dawn I got up and tried to clean myself a little. Again it was a raw misty morning. Before long two gunner officers arrived to use the house as an observation-post from which to direct a few rounds of shell-fire, but luckily brought no retaliation. We talked to them and shared breakfast of tea and bread and jam.

It seemed so quiet this morning that headquarters sent us orders to do salvage work. The wounded had all been brought in; the stretcher-bearers were collecting and burying the dead; I sent men to help in this and to collect arms and equipment. But during the morning it rained once more, and at times there was some shell-fire, at which the poor wretched men returned to their shell-holes. They got the worst of the weather; but we in our wooden shed right on the skyline soon began to attract the shells. The Colonials on our right were expecting trouble. Suddenly a signal went up, three little lights pale against the rainy sky, red and green and white. It was the S O S. Then both barrages fell and the "crumps" burst all about the valley. Though it turned out to be a false alarm, the artillery never altogether died away, and as the afternoon wore on, the enemy's guns searched the Stroombeek valley and the ridge whereon we were. Luckily the men in the open lower down the slope were in little danger.

§ 5

Pill-boxes had begun by being concreted cellars in farm houses; they grew gradually into keeps of reinforced concrete in the midst of the wreckage of ruined houses; in the third stage the ruins were scattered by shell-fire and the square boxes of concrete were left standing alone. We had found in the vestibule of this mansion a little kennel door leading to a tiny cellar perhaps six feet in each dimension, half its depth being below ground-level. This closet was concreted over, and being watertight, had naturally filled up to ground-level with rain-water. At some time or other it had been used as a latrine, and the smell from it was prodigious.

When a second time the S O S was sent up (as far as we could see, without reason) and again our barrage fell and the German retaliation came crashing round us, I began to look for cover. A near whizzbang decided me. Smell or no smell, I would explore the funkhole. I crawled in and found a ledge round the kennel and a few boards just above water-level stretched across the corners. It was safe from anything less than a direct hit from a 5·9. But if I let my hand drop carelessly or hung my foot over the edge of the board it fell into two feet of stagnant green water fetid and slimy sewage. The smell of it was midway between a septic tank and a tidal river in an industrial town, and it had a staleness all its own. Thorburn almost jeered when I crept into this tank, but when later in the evening a third S O S went up from the Colonials, and the shells fell closer than ever, Serjeant Walker and I went to earth together, and before long Thorburn swallowed his pride and joined us.

To-night the battalion was to be relieved. We were already far enough back not to be continually on the alert. We sat and waited from seven o'clock till midnight crouched on boards, this dank pool three inches from the seats of our trousers and the roof three inches above our heads. Since an excursion or two showed that the men were not under fire, there was nothing to do beyond exchanging a few routine messages with headquarters about the relief. We sat and talked, sticking a candle-end on a ledge to light up the slime on the damp walls and our own unshaven faces. One caller came to us, "Davy" Jones, a little racecourse tout, a man of unlimited impudence, a singer of scurrilous songs, owner of the company Crown and Anchor board, always in trouble, but always well forward in action.

For once he was beat. He had been to headquarters on some errand or other (we had made him an acting section leader) and was standing in the little trench outside when two 5·9's came over together and burst on the parapet. With that curious uncertainty of shell-fire, they had almost blown the ground from under his feet without hurting him. But he was badly shaken and had lost his impudence. We brought him into our funkhole and made a fuss of him until the shelling was over.

We soon fell into a sentimental conversation,

"Of old unhappy far-off things
And battles long ago."

Jones and I talked of our old fights, of Ovillers and Gommecourt, and the good times in summer out at rest, and of the friends who had "drawn their full issue" long before. It was Stanley that never left my mind. Although it seems a trivially selfish way to think of his death, it was the discomfort of his absence that made me think the more of his loss. He had been a part of my life for eighteen months, and through these four days I had been helpless without him. Now that we had an opportunity to think clearly, I began to realise how much was lost to me. The element of comedy about him made his tragedy the sadder. I remembered the fights we had fought together, Ovillers where he had saved half his water for me when we were all parched in the July heat, Pozières where we had lived a day and a night in one "cubby-hole" eating from the same dish, Epéhy where we wandered together among falling shells and driving snow. But more characteristic and sadder now was his grotesque face with "a smile that went up sideways, from the corner of his nostril," and I thought of his stolen ride to Amiens in my best breeches, and his cutting off the heads and cooking the stalks of the asparagus that I had gathered under shell-fire.

He had said to me a dozen times, "Why, the shell 'aint made yet with my name on it, sir."

It had always been his way to tell pointed little stories about his own behaviour in action, for he always called himself a coward, but, as I remembered, it was his advice that I had always valued most in battle, and advising me the bolder course he had been killed.

140

I thought how recently he had told me of his brother's death in action.

"Ar! 'E was a good kid, was Stanley," said Jones. "An' so was young Greenwood, and Fred Smith an' all. They was good lads, all on 'em."

There was another thing weighing on my mind as well. I began to realise that I had vaguely left a Lewis-gun section with the 16th Battalion at Winchester. Several times it had occurred to me to send for them, but I had not done so. Serjeant Walker and I were the only two men who knew their exact position, and it would be very irregular for either of us to go. Somehow, I could not make up my mind to send any of my tired handful over that dreary mile of mud under heavy fire to look for one particular shell-hole among a thousand exactly like it. I knew the 16th, to whom they were attached, would look after them, but felt very guilty nevertheless, because they had only stayed there by my own unofficial arrangement. My anxiety was not relieved when I learnt afterwards that they left the front line with the 16th later in the night under a heavy bombardment, which the rest of us, starting earlier, had avoided. We got back safely, but their section commander, third in four days to hold that position, was killed and another man was wounded. Later it sometimes seemed to me that this man's blood was on my head. But as yet I could only trust that they were not forgotten and leave them to the 16th. I sent them no message.

At last our relief came. Section by section the relieving regiment arrived and replaced each of my groups with a platoon. Thorburn saw to the section reliefs; it was my place to "hand over" company headquarters and explain the tactical situation. Each party moved off as it was relieved, till at last Serjeant Walker and I were left alone.

Reporting at battalion headquarters as we passed, we moved over the hill towards St. Julien. I was full of anxiety to cross the Steenbeek and get away, being terribly frightened of being hit now at the last minute. We passed the Winnipeg road and the old Langemarck trench line, left on our right Janet Farm, where the doctor plied his trade, then crossed the little bridge over the Steenbeek among the rusting remains of twenty-two tanks lying dead in the bottom of the valley, and reached the road, where at last there was a firm foothold to find unless you trod in a shell-hole. This road was subject to sudden gusts of shelling, but none came. Columns of mules and wagons with ammunition passed us going up to the batteries in safety. As we got up towards Vanheule Farm a few shells fell lower down the road. But here there was a pill-box, and—thank God—a soup kitchen. We drank thick soup out of old jam-tins and moved on. The company was still all in front of us, though we could travel much faster than they. Our destination was Irish Farm, and we had only the sketchiest idea where it lay.

We were just out on the road again when two or three 5.9's fell, searching along it. The nearest was very close. A motor lorry standing there jammed in its clutch and started hell-for-leather. Walker leapt to one side, I to the other.

"Let's get on board!" I shouted to him. Yelling at the driver to give us a lift, I sprang on the footboard as the lorry thundered past. Another shell crashed down. The lorry jolted on, taking shell-holes at a flying leap, doing twelve or fifteen miles an hour in black darkness. When we had gone two or three hundred yards out of danger, I discovered that I was the only passenger. Serjeant Walker must have been too slow. So I deserted him.

"Where are you going?" I asked the driver. "Anywhere near Irish Farm?"

"No, sir. St. Jean."

"Which way is Irish Farm?"

"Down Admiral's Road. Just here on the right." The corner of Admiral's Road was perhaps the most dangerous cross-roads in the salient. I dismounted and hovered about in terror, waiting for Walker, as the lorry had only taken me a few hundred yards. But he never came, and I wandered down that grisly road alone, hugging the side of it and ready to jump into the ditch if anything came over. As far as I remember, I met nothing but a solitary tank crawling stridently, uncannily towards the front.

A mile down the road other groups of men came in sight, and at last a redcap[1] at a corner guiding the converging parties towards a road leading to the left. Before long a little track led into an open field where bivouac sheets were being raised in rough grass. There was no elation of victory. Silently rum was issued and the companies settled down for the night. Serjeant Walker and all my stragglers came in.

Cold, damp and utterly despondent I crept into my valise and slept.

It seemed to me that I had been feeble, inactive, and unnerved, but for my part in this battle I was given the Military Cross and a captaincy. I had expected a court-martial.

Casualties to the Battalion:

Killed	...	4 officers,	81 other ranks.
Wounded	...	6 officers.	171 other ranks.
		10	252

[1] A military policeman.

The total, 262, being about half of those who took part in the battle. At this stage of the war, in order to avoid the disproportionate death-rate among officers, only sixteen per battalion went into action. This time ten were hit. My company set out with three officers, seventeen N.C.O.s and ninety-two men. One officer, two N.C.O.s and forty-four men survived the attack unhurt.

CHAPTER V

1917—1919

THE END OF A SUBALTERN'S WAR

How different were the days spent in rest after Passchendaele, from the happy holidays which succeeded the Battle
of the Somme, a year before. One no longer had a boy's
resilience. Two winters in the trenches had struck a chill
into our bones. Heart and nerve and sinew had served
their turn, and were most unwilling to be forced into further service. It was hard to build up B company again
when the old comrades were scattered at last. With a kind
of apathy we set to work, only spurred on a little by
medals and promotion, to re-create the old tradition; and
grew in time as fond of the new as of the old company.
War had become so normal an activity that one's mental
horizon was bounded by the British front in France and
the interval before next spring with its new battles. World-
politics swept over our heads unnoticed, and the future
meant nothing to men living in daily expectation of
death.

We went into cushy trenches near the Vimy Ridge,[1] where there had been no fighting for six months. This was good training for our new recruits, who only needed to be "shot over" before they became fit for the next adventure. which, when it came, shook us out of our apathy. We were sent off to Italy to repair the disaster which the Italians had suffered at the Battle of Caporetto. A five days' train journey through new and friendly lands, a week of marching through the plains of Lombardy in fine frosty weather, made so complete a change that as I led my company, singing "Where the Swanee River flows," through a village near Verona, and a friendly Staff officer called me by name from a window, shouting, "Good! Damned good marching! The best in the brigade," my heart swelled with pride, as if 1915 had come again.

During the winter of 1917-1918 we moved about behind the Italian front in reserve positions, seeing no more of the war than an occasional reconnaissance of the Alpine front and a few air-raids on the plains. Though I did not suspect it, the war had ended for me. Early in 1918 I was given long leave, which I spent simply and happily with cousins who did war-work in London, and after a train of accidents was sent to a reserve battalion in England, where I remained for the rest of the war. Here one's motives were strangely mixed. England was beastly in 1918; it was in the hands of the dismal and incompetent. Pessimism raged among those who knew nothing of the war; 'défaistisme," the desire to stop the war at all costs, even by the admission of defeat, broke out among the faint-hearts; while those at home who still had the will to fight preferred to use the most disgusting means—to fight by lying propaganda, and by imitating the bad tradition of the German army which consistently made war against

[1] Here we were delighted to entertain two parties of American officers, attached to us for instruction.

146

civilians. No wonder that a genuine and silent pacifism was rising in the breast of the war-weary populations. Envy, hatred, malice and all uncharitableness, fear and cruelty born of fear, seemed the dominant passions of the leaders of the nations in those days. Only in the trenches (on both sides of No Man's Land) were chivalry and sweet reasonableness to be found. How delightful was the comradeship of the trenches compared with the petty jealousy of a reserve battalion, where the staple conversation turned on the methods one's neighbours used to avoid being sent to France. In such a place the keen soldiers were inclined to form a coterie and affect a superior knowledge of world affairs. The temporaries waiting to go out with a draft of men to the trenches would despise the permanent staff, dug in, "embusqué" as the French said, in safe places in England; yet who knew in his heart which was the happier state: which "embusqué" would give his soul to go abroad, which of the others to stay at home?

At first I was downright glad to have a dry bed and a whole skin, but unrest soon seized me. Boredom was succeeded by a longing to be "with the lads." I shrank from the trenches, and then pulled strings at the War Office to get sent back to them. Meanwhile I shared a hut with a musician who had drifted into the army although he was a pacifist. He assured me he would never fire a shot or strike a blow, even in self-defence, though he had no objection to dying for his country and was, strangely, in spite of his views, a good officer. We decorated our room with impressionist pictures, and read learned books. I remember we rejoiced together over Bradley's "Shakespearean Tragedy." Then he was "sent out on a draft" and immediately killed. I have no doubt he devoted himself to death.

I sat alone in the hut, not caring much (it was too late in the war to mind a death), and sat down to write. Then the first draft of this memoir took shape, but mostly I wrote essays on tactics and read all the military experts in all the newspapers. There were also bad romantic verses about death, and the trenches, and men I had served with two years ago.

When in the summer my regiment fought a battle in the Alps, I grew directly anxious to rejoin them, and pestered the higher command with applications. As the autumn came on I was afraid of coming too late, quite dreading the thought of missing the final victory. Not till a few days before the Armistice did my orders come, and I got to Italy as the war ended.

After the Armistice there were strange doings among the armies which waited six months to be demobilised. To throw so powerful a machine out of high gear into neutral, niether stops its progress nor makes it easy to control. Life was pointless, and very few soldiers were lucky enough to know in what direction their lives would tend. Millions of young men had known no other career, no other destiny than battle. It was rather like the second act of "Othello," where a gentleman enters crying: "News, lads, our wars are done." What then? For a long time there was nothing adequate to the occasion but for "every man to put himself into triumph, some to dance, some to make bonfires, each man, to what sport and revels his addiction leads him"; or to sing with Iago:

> "A soldier's a man;
> A life's but a span;
> Why, then, let a soldier drink!"

Many of us were quite indifferent to the future. Even after being demobilised the subject of this memoir did nothing and thought very little for some weeks, until upon a Tuesday the spirit moved him to go to Oxford, and on the Friday he exchanged the fourth for the fifth age, to be not a man of action but a mere purveyor of criticisms.

> "Full of wise saws and modern instances,
> And so he plays his part."

APPENDIX A

NOTE ON TRENCH WARFARE

To be able to picture a soldier's life in France, during 1914–18, it is necessary to understand some of the principles of trench fighting. The Great War on the Western front began like most other wars with a period of open fighting, when cavalry were employed on horseback and battles were short and sharp. It then passed into a period of stalemate, when infantry and guns burrowed underground and hammered at one another in prolonged trench-to-trench battles. In reality the period of fixed trench warfare was not so long as has been generally supposed. The lines were rigid only in 1915 and 1916.

There was immense variation between one sector of front and another. The British front can be distinguished into two parts: in the north the water-logged plains of Flanders and Artois, in the south the chalk downs of Picardy, drained by the Somme and its tributaries. Trenches, properly speaking, could not long exist in Flanders, where the country is scientifically irrigated by many little water-courses. When these were damaged by shellfire the countryside rapidly turned into a morass in which it was impossible to dig. During a battle in Flanders men lived in muddy shell-holes which always tended to fill up with water. In the period of fixed trench warfare the best positions in these parts were breastworks, behind which a man could hide, thick and high walls, built up on "sandbags" which are small sacks filled with clay and laid in courses like bricks. Farther to the south in Picardy, very neatly designed trenches could be cut to any depth in the hard chalk. In most parts of the line the trenches varied between these two extremes, and life was a struggle to dry and drain and dig what the weather and the enemy's bombardment were continually destroying. To keep a trench habitable there were two necessities: a scientific drainage scheme must be planned to carry off mud and water into a deep pit (a "sump hole"); and the sides of the trench had to be prevented from falling in by "revetment," that is by lining the trench with pit props, or brushwood, or sandbags well bonded together and hammered tight with the flat of a spade. In fact, no set of trenches ever was kept in perfect condition, and the more complete were these works the more likely would it be that the enemy would observe and bombard them. It may be noticed that the Germans were far cleverer than we at trench design and repair, so that to capture a German trench usually meant to move from discomfort to comfort.

To defend a position, much more than a single line of trenches was required. When a position was occupied for any length of time an attempt would be made to complete at least two parallel trenches perhaps two hundred yards apart, a front line occupied by sentry posts, and a support line where most of the men off duty lived in dugouts. Communication trenches would be dug when time permitted from the front line back to the support line, and then farther back still until they reached a point invisible to the enemy. After two years' trench warfare some communication trenches were three miles long. If front line, support line and communication trenches were in good condition, which did not often occur, trench reliefs and working-parties could move about by day. Otherwise all movement had to be done by night and over the top. Dugouts began as mere cavities scooped into the side of a trench. Bit by bit they would be extended, lined with boards, strengthened with beams and courses of sandbags until they became more or less proof against splinters of shell. The only dugouts safe from a direct hit by a high-explosive shell were "mine dugouts," underground chambers reached by an inclined shaft made like the gallery of a coal mine. To be safe a dugout needed a shaft at least fifteen feet deep. One we observed on Mont St. Quentin began at the bottom of the vaults of a church and ran down for forty-seven steps.

To complete a trench system two more things were required: barbed wire and "strong points." A barbed-wire entanglement would be erected about twenty or thirty yards in front of each line of trenches. Three lines of posts would be hammered into the ground—in silence and darkness—and barbed wire would be criss-crossed from post to post. This simple obstacle could be strengthened by loose tangles of barbed wire coiled among the stakes or by various stock pattern wire frames, called "gooseberries," "knife-rests" and what not, which could be prepared in the trench and hastily fixed in front of it by night. Behind the support line it was important to prepare a number of strong points or redoubts. These were little fortresses designed in terms of trenches and wire, where a small permanent garrison could hold out even if the main trench lines were taken by the enemy. The endless technical work required to maintain these trenches was done by the officers and men who were holding the line, with some supervision by the Royal Engineers.

On the average the front lines of the two armies were from one to four hundred yards apart, and the middle of

No Man's Land was green and empty, since no one had occasion to bombard it. Hence in 1915 and 1916 a battle had to begin with a conventional trench-to-trench attack "over the top" (or "over the plonk" as a slang phrase of 1916 put it). First you must destroy the enemy's wire by shell-fire and make gaps in your own through which to emerge. Then at zero hour you climbed over the top of your trench, raced across No Man's Land and occupied the enemy's front line, if you could do it. Once there, the battle was sure to resolve itself into a scurry of bomb-fighting in which parties of men rushed up and down the trenches throwing bombs at one another, a most unsatisfactory employment, exceedingly unpleasant and rarely leading to decisive victory for either party. Bombs had to be used because of the tortuous plan on which trenches are always dug. If a trench were a straight ditch the enemy might be able to place themselves in such a position as to "take it in enfilade," that is, to fire along it from end to end, which is avoided by making a kink in the trench every five or ten yards. The straight lengths in which men stand up to fire at the enemy are called "bays" of a fire trench, and the kinks are called "traverses." When moving about in trenches you turn a corner every few yards, which makes it seem like walking in a maze. It is impossible to keep your sense of direction and infinitely tiring to proceed at all, squeezing past people at narrow bends, paddling through mud and water, climbing over obstructions made by shell-fire and being caught under the chin or across the ankles by trailing telephone wires to some forward signal station. It is usually in the dark that you go on this pilgrimage, and either with fifty pounds of kit on your back, or worse still, with a load of pit props, barbed wire, sandbags and corrugated iron. When trenches had been fought over, the confusion became the greater. Instead of neat parallel trench lines you made the best use of existing trenches

153

which might run in any direction other than the one you would prefer, until an old battlefield like the Somme became a labyrinth of trenches without any plan. Here you might find yourself living only twenty yards from the enemy, separated by a bomb-stop, or barricade to prevent him rushing along the trench to throw bombs at you.

The intensity of artillery fire grew so great in the middle of the war that permanent trench lines became untenable. During 1917 bomb fighting in trenches gave way to the shell-hole warfare described in the second of these episodes, and in 1918 to open fighting of the traditional kind in which tanks and cavalry played a large part.

In the British army machine-guns were very scarce when the war began. In 1915 a new light automatic weapon called the Lewis-gun was brought from the Belgians and given experimentally to front-line troops. During the Battle of the Somme, there were two per company, at Passchendaele four, and by the end of the war the number had been increased to eight. Lewis-guns were taken into the forefront of the battle, while the heavier and more reliable machine-guns of the older pattern were kept in positions where they could be treated with more respect.

Most of the artillery used in the war consisted of light field-guns drawn by horses and firing a shell weighing from fifteen to eighteen pounds at a range of two or three miles. The English field-gun was an "eighteen pounder"; the famous French "seventy-fives" and the German "whizz-bang" guns were, roughly speaking, equivalent. All these field-guns were used for firing on the enemy's front line, to make his infantry keep their heads down while your infantry advanced. They generally used shrapnel shells which burst high in the air, throwing a rain of bullets forward and downward. Clever gunnery consisted in bursting shrapnels just in front of your infantry to give them a protective screen or "barrage" of explosions, and if this

154

screen was slowly moved forward, which could be done by regularly altering the range of the guns, it was called a "creeping barrage." In trench warfare heavy guns, firing much larger and more highly explosive shells, were largely used.

These weapons were reinforced by many improvised devices. Numerous kinds of hand grenades were tried by every army: the British finally settled on the Mills bomb, an oval-shaped object which could be bowled like a cricket ball with a full pitch of thirty or forty yards. Many inventions were made for discharging bombs from a rifle to a longer range, and many kinds of trench-mortars were used for hurling larger bombs into the enemy lines, one being the gas-projector which threw a cylinder of poison gas to a distance of 800 or 1,000 yards.

APPENDIX B

THE British Expeditionary Force in France and Flanders consisted of about two million men under command of Sir Douglas Haig. Many hundreds of thousands of these were administrative troops who worked at the base camps, railways, hospitals and other depôts, without ever hearing a shot fired in anger except when there was a German air raid. The great bulk of the combatant troops were organised in about fifty infantry divisions each commanded by a major-general. At full strength an infantry division contained nearly twenty thousand men, forming a self-contained, self-supporting unit able to conduct an independent campaign. It consisted of three infantry brigades with a proper proportion of artillery, engineers, pioneers, Army Service Corps to bring up supplies, and Army Medical Corps to look after the sick and wounded. Divisions were grouped together into Army Corps as the situation demanded, and Army Corps into five Armies under the Commander-in-chief. The other combatant troops, aeroplanes, cavalry, tanks and heavy guns were not allotted to divisions but controlled by higher commanders.

The composition of an infantry brigade, of that time, can be shown by a simple table:

An infantry section was a corporal and about six men.

Four sections made a platoon commanded by a subaltern or serjeant.

Four platoons made a company commanded by a captain, who had several assistants making up his company headquarters.

Four companies made a battalion commanded by a lieutenant-colonel, who had a large battalion headquarters.

Four battalions made a brigade commanded by a brigadier, who had three staff officers at his headquarters.

The most important of these units was the battalion, which might consist of anything from five hundred to a thousand men according to the fortune of war. Even today the battalion still remains the link which binds men together permanently, whether on active service or at home.

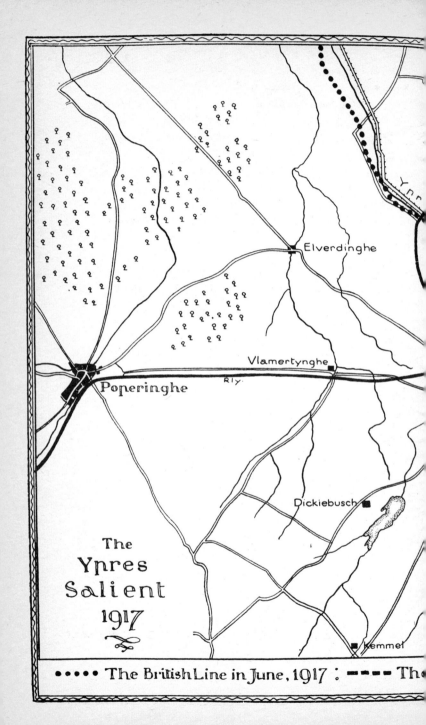

Elverdinghe

Ynr

Vlamertynghe

Poperinghe

Rly.

Dickiebusch

The
Ynres
Salient
1917

Kemmel

••••• The British Line in June, 1917 : ---- The

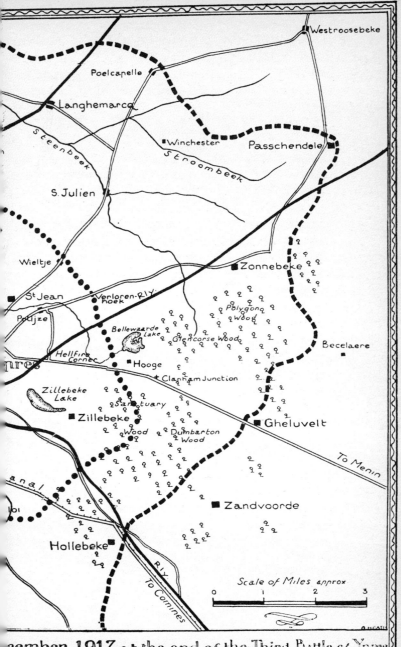

Westroosebeke

Poelcapelle

Langhemarce

Steenbeek

Winchester

Passchendele

Stroombeek

S. Julien

Wieltje

Zonnebeke

St Jean

Verloren-R.I.Y.
Hoek

Polygone
Wood

Potijze

Bellewaarde
Lake

Glencorse Wood

Becelaere

Hellfire
Corner

Hooge

Clapham Junction

Zillebeke
Lake

Sanctuary

Zillebeke

Wood

Dumbarton
Wood

Gheluvelt

To Menin

Canal

Zandvoorde

Hollebeke

R.I.Y.

To Comines

Scale of Miles approx

0   1   2   3

cember, 1917, at the end of the Third Battle of Ypres

THE WAR LIBRARY

War has been part of the human condition since the earliest battle between cavemen over the carcass of a dead animal. Our history is the history of war and some of the most remarkable books from any century are those written by men and women attempting to record and rationalise the experience of killing each other.

The aim of *The War Library* is to bring together in one series many of the finest and most enduring of these books. Whether they describe the battleground or the home front, whether they represent personal experience, reporting, or fiction the essential ingredient will be that each book has contributed something of lasting value to the literature of war.

Titles in print or soon to be published:

Old Soldier Sahib	*Frank Richards*
Old Soldiers Never Die	*Frank Richards*
Beyond the Chindwin	*Bernard Fergusson*
Going to the Wars	*John Verney*
Bengal Lancer	*F. Yeats-Brown*
A Subaltern's War	*Charles Edmonds*
War	*Ludwig Renn*
And No Birds Sang	*Farley Mowat*
Battle Sketches	*Ambrose Bierce*
Broken Images	*John Guest*
Rough Justice	*C. E. Montague*
Disenchantment	*C. E. Montague*

If you would like more information, or you would care to suggest books which you think should appear in the series, please write to me at the following address: Anthony Mott, The War Library, 50 Stile Hall Gardens, London W4 3BU.